A PADRE PIO PROFILE

A
Padre Pio
Profile

Rev. John A. Schug, Capuchin

ST. BEDE'S PUBLICATIONS
Petersham, Massachusetts

St. Bede's Publications
Petersham, MA 01366-0545

99   98   97   96   95   94   10   9   8   7

Imprimi potest: Very Rev. Gregory Reisert, Capuchin
                    January 20, 1987

Nihil obstat: Rev. Joseph Pius Martin, Capuchin
                  February 2, 1987

Imprimatur: +Timothy J. Harrington
                Bishop of Worcester
                May 21, 1987

The *Nihil obstat, Imprimi potest* and *Imprimatur* are official declarations that a book is free from doctrinal or moral error. No implication is contained herein that those who have granted them agree with the contents or opinions expressed. In presenting these interviews, the author declares his submission to the decree of Pope Urban VIII, the law of the Church, and the decrees of the Holy See.

LIBRARY OF CONGRESS CATALOGING-IN-PUBLICATION DATA

Schug, John A.
    A Padre Pio profile.

    1. Pio, padre, 1887-1968. 2. Capuchins—Biography.
I. Title.

BX4705.P49S383   1987   271´.36´024 [B]   87-16664
ISBN 0-932506-56-9

Contents

To Padre Pio,
the Wise Man
of the Gargano

Preface

Padre Pio was a Capuchin Franciscan priest who for fifty years bore the stigmata, the wounds of Jesus, in his hands and feet and side. Born in 1887 in Pietrelcina, near Naples, most of his priestly ministry was in the small town of San Giovanni Rotondo, which hangs precariously onto the Gargano Mountain just above the heel of the Italian boot. His life span of eighty-one years bridged the "old" Church and the "new" Church after the Second Vatican Council. He died on September 23, 1968.

Popes, not often given to flights of fancy, extolled him. As far back as 1921, Benedict XV called him "truly a man of God." Pius XI asked his advisor Don Orione to investigate the rumor that Padre Pio had appeared in the Vatican through bilocation (the ability to be in two places at one time). Don Orione reported: "I have seen him myself!" The Pope replied: "If you tell me that, then I believe it." (The same Don Orione was subsequently beatified by Pope John Paul II.)

Giulio Antonaci, major general of the carabinieri, had an audience with Pius XII, along with high-ranking air force officers, Bishops, nuns, and religious groups. Antonaci used the occasion to request a special audience for twenty of Padre Pio's spiritual children. Bishop Montini, then the Pope's secretary and later Pope Paul VI, said in a loud clear voice: "Padre Pio is a saint." A Bishop nearby snapped: "Post mortem!" Pius XII heard the exchange and said with a smile and a grand gesture: "No, no dear Excellency. We all know that Padre Pio is a saint even before he has died."

Later Montini, as Pope Paul VI, called Padre Pio a "marked representative of the stigmata of Our Lord" (*era, difficile a dire, representante, stampato, delle stigmate di nostro Signore*).

As this book goes to press, Pope John Paul II is planning to visit San Giovanni Rotondo on May 23, 1987, and pray at the tomb of Padre Pio. This will be the Pope's third visit to San Giovanni Rotondo. The first occasion was in 1949, when as a student priest in Rome he visited and confessed to Padre Pio. When he was Cardinal Archbishop of Krakow, he again visited San Giovanni Rotondo to pray at Padre Pio's tomb. Also while he was still Cardinal Archbishop, the National Conference of Polish Bishops unanimously petitioned Pope Paul VI to canonize Padre Pio. The second name on the petition, after that of the Primate Cardinal Wyszynski, was that of Karol Wojtyla.

The devotion of the present Pope to Padre Pio is no secret. Padre Pio had predicted his election as Pope, and also that he would shed his blood as Pope. Television cameras captured the fulfillment of the latter prophecy on May 31, 1981, when Mehmet Ali Agca pumped four bullets into the unsuspecting pontiff in St. Peter's Square.

In 1983 Pope John Paul II spoke for fifteen minutes to 20,000 members of Padre Pio's Prayer Groups from all over the world meeting at St. Peter's. He departed from his prepared speech to recall his two visits to San Giovanni Rotondo. "I have been able to meet the Servant of God," he told the throng of people. "During my priestly life, I was able to meet him personally in the forties. I was also able to confess to him, and as a Cardinal I was able to visit again."

On the same day, Cardinal Sabatini presided at a Mass for the 2,000 Prayer Groups concelebrated by no less than three hundred priests. He reminded them that the Pope himself "is also witness to a prodigious cure of a person well known to him." The Cardinal was referring to a letter that the Pope had written to Padre Pio in 1962 before having become Pope, in which he asked Padre Pio to pray for "a forty-year-old woman, a mother of four, who spent five years in a Nazi concentration camp. Her life is now in danger because of cancer." Padre Pio confided to Angelo Battisti (the administrator of his hospital): "I cannot say no to this." Eleven days later Bishop Wojtyla wrote again to Padre Pio to tell him: "The woman from Krakow, the mother of four girls, was instantly healed. Thanks to God. And I thank you, too, venerable Father."

The Vatican newspaper *L'Osservatore Romano* reported this meeting of the Prayer Groups. "Incessant prayer," said the article, "is the scope and essence of the spiritual movement of the Padre Pio Prayer Groups, which have a good 200,000 members in almost all the world."

Since the 1920s the media have been attracted to Padre Pio. In 1967 the United Press International estimated that a million and a half people visited him in that year alone. Documentaries by ABC News, the BBC, and a two-hour Swiss film clearly show Padre Pio's stigmata as he offered Mass. Another film, "Fifty Years of Thorns and Roses," has been viewed by many thousands of people.

William F. Buckley Jr.'s prestigeous *National Review* ran a two-page feature article in February, 1968: "The Phenomenon of Padre Pio." When Padre Pio died in September of that year, the same magazine ran a full page obituary. Farley Clinton called Padre Pio "the hottest thing in mysticism in the twentieth century."

My dear Lutheran friend Pastor C. Bernard Ruffin, author of the best-seller, *Padre Pio: The True Story*, said: "Padre Pio was certainly, if a tenth of what has been written and testified about him is half true, a charismatic in the New Testament sense of having a staggering abundance of spiritual gifts, or charisms."

The Catholic Church has long been familiar with saints, mystics, social apostles, and fantastic charismatic phenomena. But I know of no other person in history who has had such a range of gifts encapsulated within himself or herself. There has never been anyone like him. Thus I see Padre Pio as a man with a rele-vance and importance—and a message—to the whole modern world, from Catholics to atheists.

Can any journalist's pen do justice to the sweep of the seemingly infinite panorama of Padre Pio's eighty-one years among us? I think not. Biographies (including my own *Padre Pio*), and magazine articles abound in many languages. They tell much about the man, but I think they only scratch the surface. Perhaps that tide is changing. Padre Pio's *Letters*, now available in English (1,300 pages in the first volume alone), are beginning to show the world an unsuspected depth of his mysticism which at least equals that of Teresa of Avila and John of the Cross.

Until now nobody has ever published in a single volume the interviews that are actually the source material of the biographies—interviews of a broad range of people who knew him personally: his Capuchin superiors and confreres who lived with him, his personal physician, farmers, shopkeepers, politicians and pilgrims. I call these people the first generation of Padre Pio's spiritual children.

For lack of space I have had to exclude from this book my interviews of people who, although they might have met him, confessed to him, and received miracles from him, did not actually live under his thumb. I call these people the second generation of his spiritual children.

This book, therefore, is not another biography. It is the firsthand source of facts and personal encounters with Padre Pio upon which biographers have drawn. Most the persons whose interviews are in this book are of the first generation of Padre Pio's spiritual children, and they speak of their own experience. To my surprise, during my interviews they were tightlipped about stories they had heard from others, incidents in which they themselves had not been personally involved.

I met almost all of them through the kind help of Father Alessio and Father Joseph Pius, Capuchin priests who lived with Padre Pio and are still stationed in San Giovanni Rotondo. For two months during my first visit in 1971, and during several subsequent visits, they gave me time which they could ill afford. They allowed me to interview them, too. Although I was not required by law to obtain their approval, I know the sensitivity of the Capuchins to the truth. They do not want legends to grow up about this man concerning whom truth is stranger than fiction. They were grateful, therefore, for the chance to preview my manuscript, and I was grateful for this additional sacrifice of their precious time.

One strange phenomenon that I experienced (you may detect this as you read the interviews) is the similarity of the statements, almost as if each individual's description of the same incident had been rehearsed. I can assure you that there has never been any such orchestration. Nor can I explain the similarity of style that you might detect in these printed interviews. They are my re-writing of their stories "as told to Father John Schug." Of course I had to do some editing of my forty hours of interview tapes. However, my own input is minimal. These interviews are theirs, not mine.

While I was conducting my interviews, perhaps the strangest phenomenon was that never once did language present a problem. I traveled from San Giovanni Rotondo in southern Italy, to Alessandria in the north, then across to Palermo, Sicily, and as far as Budapest, Hungary. Almost all of the interviews were in Italian. I still cannot speak or understand Italian. Remarkably, whenever I needed a translator, I had one.

A few times I thought I would miss an interview because no translator was available. But in those cases Padre Alessio would telephone ahead to the persons I wanted to see. He explained to them what I wanted and set up the interview. Then I visited them with my tape recorder and simply let them talk. When I returned to the United States, my Italian-speaking friends translated the tapes for me. Among these translators, I owe a special debt of gratitude to Phylomena Colasuonno.

Some of the stories in this book have never been told before. I can understand why. The people with whom I spoke, although they were knowledgeable about Padre Pio, were reluctant, and sometimes almost refused, to speak about anything extraordinary. They knew well that Padre Pio's charismatic gifts, even the stigmata, did not make him a saint. Jesus makes us saints, through His Sacraments, and through our outreach in prayer and sacrifice. So when I met them, they would ask me how they could attend Mass more devoutly and pray the rosary more fruitfully. That was how "their priest" spoke to them, and that was how they expected a priest to speak to them today. All the rest—Padre

Pio's miracles, bilocation, reading of their souls—they did not want even to talk about these phenomena.

Some readers may never have read a biography of Padre Pio. Therefore, when background information might be necessary, I will add a note in brackets. The introductory notes in italics that introduce each interview are my own.

When the same incident is described by several persons, I beg the reader not to say: "I have heard this before." Rather, I ask you please to look on the second account as testimony from a different and independent perspective. Then what might seem to be mere duplication actually gives the story an element of even greater significance. I think that the corroboration of stories ought not be lost to history. As these interviews evolve, I think that a portrait of Padre Pio will emerge.

I am grateful to the Benedictine Sisters of St. Bede's Publications, who have accepted this manuscript. Perhaps Padre Pio is smiling on this joint Capuchin and Benedictine venture. On one occasion, before his operation for a hernia, the doctor wanted to give him an anesthetic. Padre Pio refused, so the doctor insisted that he accept at least a drink of Benedictine brandy. Padre Pio refused that, too. Playing on the words, he said: "Maybe the Capuchin and the Benedictine will get into a scuffle." Certainly there is no scuffle between the Benedictine Sisters and Padre Pio, nor between them and me.

I acknowledge a great debt of gratitude to Antonio Ciccone, the artist whose pictures appear on the cover and frontispiece of this book. Born in San Giovanni Rotondo, he was schooled in Florence by Annigoni and Simi. Without doubt he is the foremost portrait artist today who captures the presence and spirit of Padre Pio in his paintings and drawings. He knew Padre Pio personally, loved him dearly, and now has donated these drawings to his memory.

The name Padre Pio is Italian. Padre means Father, the title of respect given to Catholic priests all over the world. People everywhere continue to use his Italian title Padre and do not translate it into their own language. Pio is the Italian name of his patron saint: Saint Pope Pius V. It is his religious name, that is, the name of a new patron saint that he received when he joined the Capuchin Order. His baptismal name was Francesco Forgione.

The Capuchin Order is one of the three branches (along with the Observants and the Conventuals) of the Franciscan Order founded by St. Francis of Assisi. The Capuchins emerged as an independent reform branch of the Franciscan Order in 1528. Today almost 13,000 Capuchin friars form the fourth largest Order of priests and brothers in the world.

Padre Pio's writings, and other books, magazines, and pamphlets are available in several languages. A third-class relic, attached to a prayer card with Padre Pio's favorite novena, is also available. They may be obtained by writing to Mrs. Vera M. Calandra, The National Center for Padre Pio, Inc., 11 North Whitehall Road, Norristown, PA 19403 USA. She also lectures extensively and conducts tours to San Giovanni Rotondo.

A PADRE PIO PROFILE

1. Padre Lino, Capuchin
San Giovanni Rotondo

Father Lino Barbati was the vice-postulator for the cause of Padre Pio. I began my interview with questions about the canonization process. Since that time, however, major steps have been taken by the Vatican. Therefore, I have incorporated Padre Lino's comments with current developments in the last chapter of this book: "Canonization." Padre Lino died on September 30, 1980. His last words were cited in the Analecta, *the official international bulletin of the Capuchin Order: "Oh, the Blessed Mother. . . . Oh, how beautiful she is!" The Home for the Relief of Suffering, which Padre Lino speaks of, is a hospital built through the direct initiative of Padre Pio. Often it is called "The Casa," from the Italian title it bears:* Casa Sollievo della Sofferenza. *He did not want it to be called a hospital. "A hospital," he said, "is a place of suffering. This will be a home for the relief of suffering." Today it has almost one thousand beds. The* New York Times *printed a lengthy article on the Casa and called it "one of the most beautiful as well as one of the most modern and fully-equipped hospitals in the world."—JS*

* * *

My whole family is indebted to Padre Pio. In 1947, I was ready to offer my First Mass, and I told Padre Pio that I dreaded going back home, because my sister was gravely sick with tuberculosis, my mother had terminal cancer, my brother was sick in bed, and my whole family had not been well. I told him: "I've been away from home for thirteen years, and now that I am ready to go back to sing my First Mass, I dread it. It seems that by going home I'm going into a hospital. Everyone is sick. I am so depressed about it all."

Padre Pio said: "Take courage. Don't worry. Your sister is going to be well. She is going to be well. You will see—she is going to give you a party for your First Mass. And your brother too will be up and around. Everything is going to be just fine. You wait and see."

You know, that is just how it happened. I went back home, and after my First Mass my sister gave me a wonderful party. My brother was up and around. Everything was just wonderful, just as Padre Pio had predicted.

Then Padre Pio told me: "Tell your sister to throw away all that medicine. It is no good. Just throw it away." She did, and now she is perfectly well.

[*Padre Pio seldom offered advice like this. Almost always he insisted: "Go to the doctor and do what he tells you to do."*]

In 1959, my mother had to have surgery for a tumor and, naturally, I was very disturbed. I went to Padre Pio and asked him to intercede. Instead of operating on her, the doctors started giving her cobalt treatment. She was getting well. One day I went to Padre Pio and said: "You know, Padre Pio, those cobalt treatments are really helping my mother a great deal."

He threw his arms up in the air and said: "Cobalt! Cobalt, he says!" He made me realize that it wasn't the cobalt that had cured my mother; it was his intercession.

You asked me about Padre Pio's wounds. About three months before his death, Padre Pio's wounds had practically stopped bleeding. After his death—almost at the moment of his death—the wounds receded from his body. We can see how this happened from the photographs that Padre Giacomo took. As the body got colder, the wounds receded and closed up. The skin of his hands and feet became as smooth as a baby's skin, with no trace of blood, and then the wounds disappeared completely.

With regard to Padre Pio's accomplishments and plans, when the Home for the Relief of Suffering was dedicated, the hospital bulletin listed the so-called "works" that Padre Pio wanted. They are many: the hospital itself, the Stations of the Cross, and hospitals for spastic and retarded children. There are to be seminaries, houses for religious, houses of study, houses for retired priests, places for spiritual children and for the Prayer Groups. There is going to be a "city on the mountain." It is going to be called the "religious and medical center of Europe."

Padre Pio prayed that the Prayer Groups would become beacons of light and love throughout the world. We see that today—in the United States, Germany, England, Ireland, France, Switzerland, Sri Lanka, the Philippines—all over the world. [Registered at the Casa Sollievo Della Sofferenza, the Prayer Groups are associations of lay men and women. There are almost 2,000 of these groups around the world, with 200,000 members.]

2. Padre Bonaventura, Capuchin
San Giovanni Rotondo

In his fifty active years as a Capuchin priest, Padre Bonaventura was a famous preacher in Naples. He was eighty years old when I interviewed him. We spoke in Latin. His mind was still sharp and his eyes filled with tears at his recollections of Padre Pio. He spoke of bilocation, the ability to be in two places at one time. Padre Pio seldom left the friary, and for the last fifty years of his life he never left San Giovanni Rotondo; yet he has been seen in countries around the world.—JS

* * *

I came to San Giovanni Rotondo off and on for twenty years. I visited Padre Pio in his room, and I saw the wounds in his hands clearly, as he was washing his hands and face.

One day, in 1956 I was preaching in the Basilica of the Holy Spirit in Naples, at 7:00 p.m. There in the basilica I saw him appear, visibly, through bilocation. Not only I, but all the people saw him. They became very excited over this marvel. At first he appeared in the middle of the basilica and remained for a while in silence while I preached. Gradually he came up closer to me, with his cowl up [the hood of his Capuchin habit] and his hand in his breast pocket. He remained in that position for about forty minutes, standing there visibly in the principal nave, on the floor of the basilica. He stood there in contemplation as he listened to my prayer. All the people saw him.

Afterwards Padre Pio confirmed it. I wrote to Padre Carmelo, the superior of his friary, and I told him about the extraordinary event which had happened.

Padre Carmelo thought that I was hallucinating. He didn't believe me. But the idea stuck in his mind. One night he couldn't sleep, so he went to Padre Pio's room and asked him: "Is Padre Bonaventura right—that he saw you in the basilica?"

Padre Pio said: "Yes, it is true. It is true."

3. Mr. & Mrs. Giuseppe Scatigna
Palermo

This is a bittersweet story. I interviewed Giuseppe Scatigna in San Giovanni Rotondo in 1971. He was the picture of health, apparently cured of terminal cancer in 1968. In 1978, when I returned for a visit, I learned that he had died of cancer, but a cancer unrelated to his previous disease.

In 1968, after Giuseppe's cure, Mrs. Scatigna began to assemble documents (affidavits, biopsies, etc.) to prove her husband's miraculous cure through the intercession of Padre Pio. There was a possibility that his cure would be submitted to the Vatican as part of the cause for Padre Pio's canonization. However, because of Giuseppe's death through cancer, it seems that his case will not be considered. The Vatican will not look into a miracle if a disease has recurred in the same person, even if the second illness was unrelated to the first.

Still, everything that happened before Giuseppe's death is true. In 1978 I met Mrs. Scatigna and Rosaria, her niece, in San Giovanni Rotondo at Padre Pio's crypt. Although they grieved for Giuseppe, they were happy and proud to continue to look on Padre Pio as their beloved Spiritual Father.

Here is the account of Giuseppe Scatigna's cure, told to me when I interviewed him and his wife, and little Rosaria.—JS

* * *

In June 1966, my husband contracted cancer. It began as a little black spot on his left knee, a mole which he had had since birth. By now it had caused a tumor within his knee. The doctors were convinced that it was a simple angioma [tumor] which could be cured by surgery, so they removed the whole growth. The suture healed and no one spoke of it any more.

Two years later, in June 1968, my husband began to notice a red spot and a slight swelling in his left groin. It became more and more disturbing. The doctors thought that it was only an impacted lymphatic gland and prescribed salves, then compresses and injections of cortisone and other remedies. But it was very painful and didn't go away. There was no obvious injury or infection which had produced it. Rather than decrease, the gland increased in size and hardness and caused severe pain. It resisted all therapy suggested by the physicians.

On October 23, exactly thirty days after Padre Pio's death, the pain became intense. My husband refused to touch any food, and his temples became more and more sunken from day to day. He agreed to go back to the hospital.

On this one point the doctors all agreed: an operation was necessary. They were doubtful that it was a malignant tumor. They opened his groin and learned that they had been completely wrong in their diagnosis. He had a tumor which they should not have touched. They removed the tumor which was a big as a lemon, with roots that went very deep. It was attached to a smaller tumor which they also removed.

The histological examination was performed by Doctor Craxi at the Institute of Pathological Anatomy. His report was agonizing: "Metastasis melanosarcoma of the lymph glands." When cancer arrives at that point of metastasis, it is in the last stage and is beyond hope.

They discharged him from the hospital even before the stitches were healed. This led him to become suspicious. We were trying to keep him from understanding how bad his condition was, but he understood that we were lying to him. He said to me: "If they are sending me home in this condition, there is no hope for me. You know the truth, and I know the truth, too."

I asked my husband: "Do you want to go to Padre Pio's hospital?"

He said: "I understand. You don't want to take me to Padre Pio's hospital, but to Padre Pio himself, because only a miracle can cure me."

With my soul torn, but with a heart full of faith, we reached the Home for the Relief of Suffering, where my husband had X rays and a clinical examination. Doctor DeLuca was very brusque but truthful to me. "I am receiving him only out of charity, because a man in this condition is not supposed to stay here. There is nothing except a miracle that can save him. You already know that we have agreed that your husband should come here simply to bring him some comfort, because the diagnosis and the state he is in has left no hope. If your husband agrees to tests, we will perform them, and we will X-ray every part of his body. But have no illusion about this. Concerning the condition of your husband, there is really nothing more that science can do. I am sorry to be frank, but it is my duty to speak plainly."

My husband and I had been taking care of my niece, Rosaria (Rosariuccia—little Rosaria), whom we love as a daughter. She was born during the earthquake in Sicily. She calls us mama and papa. My husband said: "I don't mind dying, but it is very painful for me not to see this little child grow up. I feel bad that I can't bring up this child. Why am I going to abandon her?" He wept at the very thought of leaving her.

He was in the hospital between November 8 and November 13, 1968. As for me, I divided my time between the hospital and the crypt [beneath the church, where Padre Pio is buried]. All the time I was crying and crying and crying. At the same time my husband had a very brief vision. He saw Padre Pio trying to lift an enormous stone. Young people stood around laughing at him, saying: "How can he lift this enormous stone? It is impossible."

My husband said to me: "You see, Padre Pio can't do anything for us, because we're not asking for a miracle—we're asking for the resurrection! It is impossible for him to give us this one. Yet you keep asking for a miracle."

One day I went to the friary and asked Padre Carmelo, the superior, that he and all the community offer special prayers for my husband. He felt sorry for me. He said: "Your husband is dying." But he was so touched by this tragedy that he went to Padre Pio's room and brought me a piece of cloth with the blood of Padre Pio on it. He said: "I don't do this for just anybody. What I am doing is absolutely forbidden. But take this and go to your husband and put it on the sick part of his body. I don't know what more I can do."

Exultant in having such an incomparable treasure, I rushed to the hospital to show the relic to my husband. I went into his room and said: "This is from Padre Pio. Put it on the wound."

That same evening Doctor DeLuca came in. He said: "In your room are all the X rays, but please don't show them to your husband. They show the very worst. You shouldn't give him this pain. I repeat, he has only two days of life."

The following morning, November 13, 1968, Doctor DeLuca called me, and at my request he inspected the X rays and the other tests. My heart was pounding. He answered me: "Neither from these X rays nor from the other analyses do I see anything wrong."

I didn't let him finish speaking. I suddenly exclaimed: "Then Padre Pio has finally worked this miracle!"

The doctor said: "Madam, you forget that I am only a doctor and not a saint."

I asked him: "What do you advise me to do? I am talking to you not like a doctor but as if you are my brother."

He said: "Look. In the condition in which I see your husband, there is nothing I can do. It is too late. So don't take him to another hospital. If you feel in your heart that he is getting well, and that Padre Pio has helped him, and has made a miracle for him, then take him home. As a physician I can only suggest that your husband should have periodic tests. As for you, continue to have faith. I wish you good luck. Just take your husband and go home."

The doctor went straight to my husband's room and asked him: "How do you feel?"

He answered: "I feel perfectly well. I don't feel that I have been sick." In that moment he forgot that he had been so sick.

The doctor asked again: "But are you sure? Do you think it is possible for you to get up and walk?"

"Yes, I can."

"Do you think it is possible for you to go home?"

"Yes!" My husband felt perfectly well.

"All right," the doctor said, "take your suitcase and go home." That same day the doctor signed the paper discharging my husband from the hospital.

The first thing we did was to go to the friary to thank the superior. I told him: "Father, if it is true that my husband is completely cured, as we think, I have made a promise to give you one million lire [$15,000] toward the process of beatification. I'll bring you that money as soon as I go home and return here."

Padre Carmelo said: "What you need to do is just keep the faith you have in your heart, because you have more faith than ten nuns put together. What you are supposed to do now is go home with your husband. That is all." We went back to Sicily.

This happened on November 13, 1968. From that day to this, my husband has never experienced pain in any part of his body. He began to eat with a good appetite and regained and surpassed his normal weight. His face lost its cadaverous color, and the hollows in his face disappeared. He got around, did his work, and never spared himself. He has had many other examinations, every six months, but everything is negative. He takes no medication of any sort.

With us today on this visit to San Giovanni Rotondo is Rosariuccia, our niece, and I'd like to tell you an interesting story about her. One Saturday morning, November 30, 1968, between 9:00 and 9:30 a.m., I was in the pantry of the Casa del Fanciullo Padre Pio, where I worked [a home for needy children, under the patronage of Padre Pio], along with the cook, Frances Siragusa. We had been there for about a half hour, busy putting the finishing touches on the preparations for the day. Rosariuccia, who was then about twenty-two months old, was with us, standing in the corner near the door of the pantry that opens into the kitchen. Suddenly she came running with her hands extended as a child will do to meet or embrace someone. She was calling out "Pape Pio! Pape Pio! Pape Pio! Pape Pio! I'm running with open arms."

Her face was red. Her eyes sparkled. They did not express any fear. It was absolutely beautiful. At that moment she looked like an angel. She was all excited, looking through the boxes, trying to find somebody who was there. She saw somebody. I remained as if nailed to the spot, amid the bags of potatoes and cans of oil. I could not move or speak or even think. I stood still as a statue. I understood that the baby had seen something, because she was so excited.

I regained my composure and I questioned her: "What has happened to you? What are you talking about? What are you looking for?"

Rosaria, in a sharp clear voice, replied: "I have seen Pape Pio." For the first time in her life she used the verb in the proper way: "I have seen Pape Pio."

"Where did you see him?" I asked again.

She immediately pointed to the corner of the pantry where I was standing and pointed out the exact spot where she saw Padre Pio. She kept whispering: "In the corner. I have seen him."

"What did he look like?" I insisted.

"I saw him lifted up," she answered.

"Where did you see him?" I asked again.

In the pantry there was no picture of Padre Pio, nor of any other saint—only a little ceramic Madonna almost hidden by the cheese and ham. So there was nothing that could influence the child to talk and act that way. And she was only twenty-two months old! In fact, right from the time she said she saw Padre Pio, whenever I asked her to tell the story to others, she would always use the very same words and the same gestures without any change whatsoever.

Then, to my amazement, the child turned around. She went back and positioned herself near the door of the pantry in the only way she could see someone in the corner. She said: "Here." Then, turning toward the corner, she began to sort out the boxes of tomatoes and to discard them as if she were looking for something which she could not find.

Several days passed. The priest who is the founder of the Casa del Fanciullo, Don Vito Bonadonna, showed Rosaria a picture of

Padre Pio. He said: "Do you know who this is?"

She said: "This is Pape Pio. But the little angels are not here."

The priest said: "What do you mean—the angels?"

She said: "Yes, there were two angels, here and here." With her finger she pointed to the right and left of the picture of Padre Pio. In the same moment I could see the baby's eyes smiling and flashing in the same way they did on that morning of November 30, when her face seemed to be aglow.

The priest said: "But there are no angels in this picture."

She took the picture and went back to the place where she saw him and said: "Here and here were two little angels. And here Pape Pio was lifted up."

The priest wanted to know what kind of angels they were. But also he kept trying to get the child to change her version of the story. He said: "What were they doing? Dancing?"

The child kept quiet. She was getting nervous and didn't say a word—after all, she was only twenty-two months old. The priest said: "Tell me something. How were they dressed? Did they have wings?"

She said: "Those—no, no wings at all. Those angels did not."

About a month later a Carmelite priest, Padre Sylvestro Scalzo, was with us. He had heard of the child and took her back to the pantry and had her repeat every word she had said that morning. Then when they rejoined us, he began to tease the little child and purposely questioned her to see if she would change her story. The child would not yield. She repeated herself consistently, using the same words.

Suddenly he asked her: "Tell me—the little angels that you saw—did they have wings?"

He was expecting a definite yes. Instead, the child answered flatly: "No, they did not have wings."

When at the end the priest was ready to leave, he went near the child to say goodbye. The little girl was afraid to be questioned again. She waved her little hands excitedly and blurted out: "Oh, my—this Padre Sylvester," as if to say: "I can't take any more of this."

4. Margherita Hamilton
Rome

When I visited Miss Hamilton in her home in Rome she was eighty-one years old. This interview gave me more than I had anticipated. I met not only Miss Hamilton, but at her side was her dear friend, the Marquise Giovanna Boschi. Both ladies were among the most devoted—and uniquely blessed—of Padre Pio's spiritual daughters.

My jaw dropped as I listened to Margherita describe, quietly and calmly but with obvious deep feeling, the strangest story I had ever heard about Padre Pio—a story involving both Margherita and Giovanna.

The story is this: At 2:30 in the morning of September 23, 1968, Giovanna actually appeared inside the Capuchin friary of San Giovanni Rotondo, at Padre Pio's bedside, as he lay on his deathbed.

Preposterous? Perhaps. Personally I believe her.

I feel that I must preface her amazing account with two independent statements: one by Padre Pio himself, and another by Padre Alberto, a lifelong confrere of Padre Pio. Their statements substantiate Margherita's otherwise strange saga (over and above her own veracity and mental balance). After you have read her interview, you may wish to return to this introduction to piece the events together again.

First, the statement by Padre Pio. It is a letter he wrote to Padre Agostino, his spiritual director. He had not yet been ordained; he was Fra Pio, a Capuchin seminarian. Padre Agostino read his letter and showed it to Giovanna. She then spoke to Padre Pio, who confirmed its authenticity. Fra Pio wrote:

Several days ago I had an extraordinary experience. About 11:00 o'clock in the evening [January 18, 1905], Brother Anastasio and I were in the chapel. Suddenly I found myself at the same time in the palace of an extremely wealthy family. The master of the house was dying just as his daughter was about to be born.

Then the Blessed Mother appeared, and, turning to me, said: "I am entrusting this unborn child to your care and protection. Although she will become a precious jewel, right now she has no form. Shape and polish her. Make her as brilliant as you can, because one day I would like to adorn myself with her."

I replied: "How can this be possible? I am only a poor seminarian and don't even know whether I will have the joy and good fortune to become a priest. Even if I do, how will I ever be able to take care of this girl, since I will be so far away from her?"

The Blessed Mother admonished me: "Don't doubt me. She will come to you, but first you will find her in the Basilica of St. Peter's in Rome." After that I found myself back in the chapel.

Now, the statement by Padre Alberto. We can rely on its credibility from the fact that it was printed in the Voice of Padre Pio, *a magazine published by the Capuchins in San Giovanni Rotondo. In the article, Padre Alberto concealed the name of Giovanna by using the letters "G.R." This is his article:*

"The father of G.R. had been a registered and practicing member of the Masonic Order in Udine. As his death became imminent, his fellow Masons surrounded the palace day and night to keep any priests from entering to confess him. A few hours before he died, while his pious wife was tearfully praying beside his bed, she saw the figure of a Capuchin friar leave the room and disappear down one of the corridors of the palace. Immediately she went after him, but he had vanished.

"At that moment, sensing the approaching death of the master within the palace, the watchdog that was tied outside began to howl. Unable to bear the mournful sound, the lady went downstairs toward the door with the intention of letting him loose. Suddenly and unexpectedly, without any pain or complications, she gave birth to a baby girl. Only the steward was present to assist her. Afterwards she even had the strength to carry her prematurely-born daughter upstairs to her bed.

"The steward knew that outside of the palace a priest was trying to pass through the line of Masons in order to hear his master's Confession. Therefore, using the birth of the premature baby as an excuse, he went outside and told them: 'You have the right to keep a priest from going to the bedside of my master because he is one of you, but you cannot prevent him from entering to baptize the premature baby that has just been born inside.'

"As a result, the Masons permitted the priest to enter the palace. He proceeded directly to the dying man's room, where he helped him straighten his affairs with Our Lord and confess. A few moments later he died, begging God to have mercy on his soul.

"After her husband's death, the widow and her infant daughter went to Rome to live with her parents. The little girl grew up without ever hearing of Padre Pio or learning of the divine plan that was to guide her life. Although she received a good religious education, when she was in high school her faith was tested by a number of her teachers who did not believe in God. To make matters even worse, she knew no priests that were well enough versed in theology to answer her questions. Then late one summer afternoon in 1922 she went to St. Peter's to confess. Unfortunately at that time no priests were hearing Confessions. The custodian suggested that she return the following day since the church was about to close. . . .

"No sooner had the custodian walked away when she saw a young Capuchin friar coming toward her. 'Father, please let me confess to you,' she pleaded.

"The priest assented and entered the second confessional from the door on the left side of the basilica. After making her Confession, G.R. asked him to clarify a question she had about the mystery of the Trinity. . . . Elaborating upon this mystery of faith, the confessor was easily able to dissipate the doubts that had troubled the girl. G.R. happily left the confessional and waited to thank him, but he did not come out.

"Soon the custodian approached and told her that since the church was about to close she would have to leave but could return the next day if she wished to confess. She replied that she had just finished making her Confession and was only waiting for the priest in order to thank him. Pointing to the confessional, she indicated that the Capuchin Father who had confessed her was inside. When the custodian went to see for himself who the priest was, he opened the door . . . and found the confessional empty. 'You see, lady,' he said, 'there is no one here.'

"Bewildered, she exclaimed: 'Where can he be? I have not moved from this spot and have not seen him come out.' Perturbed by this strange incident, she went home.

"During her summer vacation in 1923, G.R. went to San Giovanni Rotondo for the first time to see Padre Pio. . . . Despite the crowd, G.R. found herself directly in his path as he passed down the corridor. Padre Pio stopped and looked closely at her.

" 'I know you!' he said. 'You were born the same day that your father died.' He then gave her his hand to kiss (an Italian custom) and blessed her.

"The following morning her aunt, who had by this time confessed to Padre Pio, suggested that she do likewise. . . . After giving her his blessing, Padre Pio welcomed her: 'My daughter, finally you have come. I have been waiting for you for so many years!'

"Surprised, G.R. immediately replied: 'Father, you don't know me. This is the first time I have ever been in San Giovanni Rotondo. Undoubtedly you have mistaken me for someone else.'

" 'No,' Padre Pio assured her, 'I have not taken you for someone else. You already know me. Last year at the Basilica of St. Peter's in Rome you came up to me. Don't you remember? You were looking for a confessor. Then a Capuchin Father came and heard your Confession. I was that Capuchin friar.'

"G.R. was completely nonplussed by this explanation of the mysterious appearance and disappearance of the Capuchin confessor at the basilica. . . . Padre Pio explained: 'Listen, my daughter. Just before you were born, the Blessed Mother took me to your home, and I witnessed the death of your father. She indicated that through her intercession and the merits of his wife's tears and prayers, he had obtained salvation. After telling me to pray for him, Our Lady informed me that his wife was about to give birth to a baby girl and that she was placing this child under my care. My daughter,' concluded Padre Pio, 'you are my responsibility.'

"Filled with emotion, the girl began to cry. 'Father, since I have become your responsibility, please tell me how I should direct my life. Should I become a nun?'

" 'No,' replied Padre Pio, 'you should not. Come to San Giovanni Rotondo frequently. I will guide your soul, and you will live according to the will of God.'

" . . . Some time later, when Padre Pio invested her into the Third Order of St. Francis, he suggested that she take the name of Sister Jacopa. Because the name did not have a pleasant ring to her ears, she asked if she could not instead be called Sister Clare.

"Padre Pio was insistent: 'No, you shall be called Sister Jacopa.' He asked: 'Have you read the life of St. Francis of Assisi? In one chapter a noble Roman lady appeared named Jacopa dei Settesoli, whom St. Francis called the beloved mother of our Order because of her generosity and protection of the Franciscans. Just as she received the grace of witnessing the death of St. Francis, *you will be present when I die*' [my emphasis].

"Under the spiritual guidance of Padre Pio, G.R. continued along the path of virtue and developed into a pious and lovely lady. She married and raised a beautiful Christian family. Frequently she went to San Giovanni Rotondo to visit her Spiritual Father. However, for some months during the last year of his life, she was unable to do so.

"One day she heard his voice sweetly advising her, 'Come soon to San Giovanni Rotondo because I am going away. If you take too long, you will miss me.'

"By now G.R. was an elderly lady. Nevertheless she hurried to San Giovanni Rotondo with a friend and registered at a hotel there. Four days before Padre Pio's death she had the good fortune of confessing to him for the last time. When Padre Pio saw her he said, 'This will be the last time you will confess to me. I absolve you now of all the sins you have ever committed.'

"She asked, 'But why can't you hear my Confession any more?'

"He replied, 'I have already told you that I cannot because I am going away.' Finally she realized that Padre Pio was going to die, and she left the confessional with tears in her eyes.

"On the evening of September 22, 1968, Padre Pio gave his last blessing to the thousands of spiritual children who had come from all over the world to visit him on the fiftieth anniversary of his stigmata. He then retired to his room to prepare for his meeting with Sister Death.

"At this time G.R. found herself in spirit in Padre Pio's room to witness in detail the last hours of her Spiritual Father's life, as he had predicted many years before when she took the name Sister Jacopa. The pious lady saw him suffer and pray. She watched as he confessed to Padre Pellegrino and renewed his religious vows. She saw him taken from his bed to the veranda. Then she saw three doctors dressed in white administer to him. Later she watched as Padre Pio received the Anointing of the Sick.

"As she saw him die, she cried, 'Padre Pio is dead! Padre Pio is dead!'

"Her cries awakened the lady who had accompanied her and many of the people in the hotel as well. Although her friend tried to calm her, telling her that she had only had a bad dream, G.R. immediately dressed and hurried to the friary. Already a small crowd had gathered in the square in front of the church, where a Capuchin friar was officially announcing the death of Padre Pio.

"Several days later G.R. came and told me that she had witnessed the death of Padre Pio. I didn't want to believe her. Wishing to give credence to her words, G.R. told me, 'Padre Alberto, I will describe Padre Pio's room as I saw it when he was dying.'

"At this point I would like to stress the fact that before December 1969, Padre Pio's room had never been photographed, nor had any woman been permitted to enter it. Imagine my wonder when she proceeded to describe his room to the smallest detail. I could not keep from exclaiming, 'Enough! I believe that you were present in his room when he died!' "

Now, at last, I will begin my interview with Margherita Hamilton.
—JS

* * *

My closeness to Padre Pio is my closeness to Giovanna. Giovanna, always Giovanna. Giovanna Boschi. She is a marquise. Clarice Bruno, in her book *Roads to Padre Pio*, calls her Vaninna Boschi.

One of the first accounts of bilocation by Padre Pio was his appearance here in Rome. Evidently Padre Pio was in San Giovanni Rotondo. He never left that town. But he appeared to my friend Giovanna here in Rome in a very strange way. [As our interview continued, Miss Hamilton told me of Giovanna's encounter with Padre Pio in the confessional in Rome. Because I have already quoted Padre Alberto's account in the introduction of this interview, I shall not repeat it here. However, I was surprised and edified that Margherita's account, as she narrated it to me, was identical, almost to the choice of words, to the report she had given to Padre Alberto several years previously. In this identity I can see another example of the concern not only of the Capuchins but also of the laity to stick to facts, without allowing legends to evolve through embellishment of the facts.]

After Giovanna's first meeting with Padre Pio in San Giovanni Rotondo, for forty-seven years she confessed only to him. Many strange things happened to her, to us, to everybody who knew Padre Pio. Nothing very great ever happened to me personally, but the things that did happen were surely strange—like the story of the rose.

Giovanna was staying with me in my house. She slept in a big bed near the wall. There was a little table at the side of the bed. On the other side was another little table, but larger. Giovanna was in bed. She had been ill.

In the morning we went out onto the terrace. There was a magnificent rose, really a splendid rose, a big beautiful rose. She said: "Oh, give me that."

I said: "No, this is the first rose of the arbor, so you cannot have this one, because this one goes to the statue of the Madonna in my room."

The next day Giovanna was still not well. I went out, and there was another rose open, which I cut. I returned to the room and said: "Giovanna, here is your rose, because it is the second."

She said: "I will give it to Padre Pio. I'll give it to him."

"All right," I said, "it can't have a better destination."

On the little table, the one near the wall, there was a photograph of Padre Pio in a little frame. So I took a small vase and put that rose there. In the afternoon another friend of ours came and the two of us sat at one side of the bed, and the rose was there near the portrait of Padre Pio. Then our friend who had come on the visit said: "Oh, how pale Padre Pio is. I hope he isn't ill."

I said: "No, it isn't that he is pale. The photograph is a colored photograph. It is that the rose has a very strong color."

I walked around the bed and took away the rose and said: "Look, he's quite normal."

She said: "Yes, it's true. He is quite normal. It's the rose that makes him look pale."

I said: "Yes, it is the rose." I put the rose back and went back to my place. We continued to chat—the two of us in the room with Giovanna in bed.

Suddenly as we were talking, my friend who was there said: "But . . . b . . . b . . . b . . . b . . ."

I said: "What are you saying?"

She said: "Th . . . th . . . th . . . the rose!"

The rose was not there. It was no longer there in the vase.

I said: "But I put it there."

She said: "Yes," and Giovanna said: "Yes, you put it there. Perhaps it has fallen."

So we went looking for it. We even got Giovanna out of bed to see if it had fallen into the bed. But the rose had disappeared completely. It was no longer there.

Then Giovanna said: "It seems that Padre Pio has accepted it." After that, we didn't talk about it.

Almost twenty days later we went to San Giovanni Rotondo, and Giovanna went straight to Padre Pio. He was in the small guest room when she arrived. He had the rose in his hand! He had the rose in his hand! *The* rose. He said: "Thank you very much for the rose. I appreciate it very much."

Giovanna said: "Oh, Father, give it to me."

He said: "Yes, I give it to you." Now that rose is framed and is in Giovanna's house. This is one of the small things connected with Padre Pio.

Another very strange thing happened to Giovanna. She had one of the gloves of Padre Pio. One day about a year after Padre Pio had died, in a moment of enthusiasm she said: "I'll give you Padre Pio's glove, because I have other things." That's what she said, but I remained without my glove for a time.

One night she dreamed that Padre Pio was there near her, and Padre Pio said: "Why didn't you give Daisy that glove? You promised it. You must give it to her."

She said: "Father, if you want me to give it, I will give it."

He said: "You can have something else."

The next morning she appeared very sad. She said: "Take this glove. You must have it, because Padre Pio said I had promised and I must give it to you."

I said: "Thank you very much. I'll take it only because I know you have many other things of Padre Pio." I know, because she also has a Bible inscribed by him, a present from him, and many other things.

That was early in the morning. She had not yet dressed, but she came running back to my room. I said: "What has happened to you?"

"I have it!"

"You have what?"

"Padre Pio's glove!"

She had been making her bed and had pulled down the blanket. On the pillow she found another glove, exactly like mine.

There were so many instances when Padre Pio helped me, even if I cannot prove them. I know that it was he, but I cannot prove it materially. For example, the year after his death I was in San Remo with a friend. It was raining every day. One day we were at lunch when the bright sun came out. I said to her: "Let's go somewhere in France."

She said: "It's too late to go anywhere by car."

I said: "No, we'll go as far as Menton." I know all those places, but that's one where I've never stopped. It's near the frontier. Off we went.

We arrived at Ventimeglia, the town nearest the frontier. Suddenly I got thirsty, so thirsty that I could hardly speak any more. I said to my friend: "Olga, please stop. Stop as soon as you can, when you see a bar or some place where we can go in and drink something. I've got this terrible thirst."

After that I didn't even speak, because I could not. My mouth was completely dry. I couldn't understand that, because never, never in my life had that happened.

Finally when we were almost at Port San Luis, we saw a place where we could turn off and leave the car. There was a café and a souvenir shop. I said: "Go in, Olga." So we drove in.

We got out of the car and were walking to the café, when suddenly there was a terrible bang. I said: "It is a bomb!" We entered the café.

Then the proprietor came in. I asked him: "What has happened? Has someone thrown a bomb?"

He said: "Oh, no, madam." He explained what had happened. Before we stopped, there had been an enormous yellow moving van in front of us. I said jokingly to my friend: "What beautiful sightseeing here!" The only thing we saw was that enormous thing, and we were right behind it.

Behind us was another big truck which we hadn't seen. As soon as we came off the road and drove to the café, that second truck crashed straight into the other truck. As it passed, the driver shouted: "My brakes are gone!" If we had gone on, if I hadn't been thirsty, we'd have been squashed between those two big trucks.

When I heard that, I said instantly: "In this I see the hand of

Padre Pio." First of all I got thirsty, and then the thirst had gone completely. As soon as I got into the café, I was no longer thirsty.

My friend said: "What do you want to drink?"

I said: "I don't want to drink anything, but I suppose I have to drink something, since I'm the one who made us stop." The thirst had gone away instantly.

[*I asked Miss Hamilton why she attributed her rescue to Padre Pio. This is her answer.*]

Because I know that Padre Pio is always protecting us. I didn't write to anyone what had happened. When I returned, my friend Giovanna came rushing to embrace me. I said before she was near me: "It's a miracle that you see me again."

She said: "I know it."

"You know it? You can't know it."

"I know it," she said. "I dreamed of Padre Pio, and I asked how Margherita was, and he said: 'Oh, Margherita! You can thank me, because if it hadn't been for me, you would never see her again.' " He told her what had happened. She couldn't possibly have known, because I hadn't written to anyone. He told her: "If it hadn't been for me, Margherita would now be saying goodbye to you."

I can think of another occasion when Padre Pio showed himself to be the protector of his spiritual children. For thirty-five years I had suffered from spastic rhinitis. It doesn't kill you, but it takes away all the pleasure of life. It is an inflammation. It is not always present, but for a long time I suffered from that affliction every morning. When I woke up, I started sneezing and I didn't stop for two or three hours—always sneezing. My face grew swollen. I generally used seventeen handkerchiefs—big, men's handkerchiefs—every morning.

My family brought me all over the world to see doctors, but nobody knew what it was. It really changed my life. I could have been married, but I didn't want that. If I had a child and this child began to sneeze, I'd become desperate. That was one of the consequences. There were many others.

After a time I grew better, a little better. That is to say it was no longer every morning. It was once every two days, and sometimes it lasted for a long time. Then it stopped a little. It was no longer continual.

One day after I confessed to Padre Pio and knelt before him for his blessing, he put both hands on my head. But it was in such a way that I had the impression that my neck was going into my shoulders. I kissed his hand and then I went away. I never sneezed once more since that time. I mean that I never had another attack. If I'd go near a window, I'd sneeze. All persons sneeze. But that's all. I have never had another attack since then. Never. But how could I say that the allergy had stopped then and there? I had already been better than I was many years before. I know that it was he, but it is not something that can be proved.

Another time when Padre Pio helped me was when I had an abscess in my ear. Once I wrote to Mrs. Sanguinetti [the wife of Doctor Sanguinetti, the administrator of the Casa Sollievo della Sofferenza]. I told her: "I am in bed with the flu, absolutely deaf, because I have an abscess in my ear, and my eardrum has burst. I do say God's will be done, but I cannot hide from you my hope that I won't remain deaf."

She went to Padre Pio and said: "Padre, Margherita didn't say that I should tell you, but she has been in bed with influenza and she cannot hear." She read the letter to him.

He laughed and said: "Daisy, always Daisy." He recognized what she was asking, but he didn't say anything until she was going away. When she was near the door, he called her back and said: "Look here, tell Daisy that I'll pray that her hearing will not be taken away from her."

When the tympanum bursts, it takes twenty-one days to heal. After twenty-one days I could hear again, and I didn't think anything more about it.

Finally that summer I was traveling about, and I found out that there was a place in Sirmione on Lake Garda where they cure hearing defects. I said to Giovanna: "I'm going there, because if later on my hearing goes, I don't want to oblige Padre Pio to work [that is, to be a victim soul] for my hearing. I would rather go deaf than ask him to work for my hearing."

So I went there. The doctor looked at my ears, and the first thing he said was: "From this ear you cannot hear."

"Yes," I said. "I can hear!"

He said: "No, you cannot hear. You hear from the other ear, and you think you hear from this one."

"But," I said, "I hear also from the other one."

He said: "It is impossible. The audio test will tell the truth."

For the audio test, the patient is enclosed in a small place with only a glass in front. The person on the other side makes a very high tone, then a lower one, and a lower one, and so forth. The technician completed the test and gave me back the report. The two ears were almost exactly alike.

The doctor said: "Then you can hear. The audio test proves it. I can't understand it. Let me look at your ear again."

He looked at me. He said: "You cannot hear, because you have so many inflammations of the eardrum. Every time an inflammation breaks, it makes a scar. After a while the cicatrization gets harder and the drum can no longer vibrate. Your drum can no longer vibrate because it is full of those things. I cannot understand how you hear."

Then I suddenly remembered what Mrs. Sanguinetti had written to me, that Padre Pio would pray that my hearing would remain. Then I said to the doctor: "Padre Pio did this."

He said: "When you come with these reasons, there is nothing I can say." So I went away and that was all. But I know that I now hear because Padre Pio prayed for me.

[*I asked every person I interviewed how Padre Pio helped people live a more Christian life. This is Margherita's response.*]

No one went to San Giovanni Rotondo without bringing something away. No one. People changed their lives—their whole way of life. People who hadn't gone to church for years, after that went to church. This I know, this I saw, having been there I don't know how many times.

Let me tell you of our visit shortly before Padre Pio died. This is true, every word of it. But first I have to tell you something which goes before this, because it is connected to it.

Many years ago, the first time I met Giovanna, she told me that when she had been invested in the habit of the Third Order, she had asked Padre Pio what her religious name was to be. She told me: "I thought he'd call me Clare. I had that in my head. But he said: 'You will be Jacopa.' "

"Jacopa!" she answered. "I don't like that name!"

And then he said: "Don't you know that she was present at the death of St. Francis? You will be present at mine." She told me that. After that she forgot it completely. Even now she says: "I could not say he told me that, because I forgot it." But *I* remember her telling me that he told her.

When Padre Pio died, I remembered how the story of Jacopa ended—how Jacopa was present at the death of St. Francis—and then I realized the connection between Jacopa and Giovanna. Here is what happened to Giovanna.

It was September 22, 1968. Giovanna and I were in San Giovanni Rotondo. Because of the crowd on that day, both of us shared the same hotel room. It was the middle of the night when we finally got to sleep. Before that, Giovanna had been very agitated. She said: "Don't you hear the dogs? Don't you hear the dogs, how they are howling?"

I said: "No, I don't hear them." Then I sat up, and then I heard it, because previously I had my pillow around my head. I heard it, and I said: "In Tuscany we call that the howling of death." Generally when a person dies in a house, the dog does that. We heard it perfectly. We went to sleep.

At half past two she suddenly woke up, *screaming*! "The Father is ill! The Father is dying! The Father is dying!"

"Giovanna," I said, "you have had a bad dream. Please keep quiet." I looked at my watch. That is the reason how I know it was half past two.

She said: "No, no, no, no! I have seen him!"

"What have you seen?"

"I went . . . I was in his room. I saw five . . . " This I don't remember—if she told me five, or if she told me seven Capuchins were in the room.

"Three were dressed in white," she said.

"But Giovanna, how could that be?"

She said: "Oh, they evidently were doctors. They evidently were doctors, and Padre Pio is very . . . "

I asked her: "But where was Padre Pio?"

"I don't know. They were all looking down, all lined up in a straight row, looking down. He was dying." He died in that moment, which I can describe, because she described it. And to this I can testify—that she was in bed with me. So I know where she was. But she was so anxious that she said: "I must go and see."

I said: "Giovanna, please! In the middle of the night you are going out?"

She said: "I must." She put on something and away she went. I was thinking: I had better dress, because she is so excited. I will go to meet her. I was thinking something like that, but I was still in bed. All of a sudden I heard her *scream* in the distance. I heard her voice. I jumped out of bed. I didn't even have time to put my dressing gown on. I went through the hall of the pensione [rooming house], opened the door, and went into the garden. I saw her arrive there, screaming: "The Father is dead, the Father is dead. We are lost persons, orphans! We are orphans! We will never have him again!"

When I heard "The Father is dead," I said to myself: My God, now she will have a heart attack. But I had no time to think of that, because she was coming toward me. I rushed to her and took her into my arms and said: "Giovanna, keep still! You mustn't howl this way. You will disturb the whole lot."

I grabbed her and threw her, really, onto the bed and then started scolding her. I said: "I don't know, I don't think that the Father is dead, but if he is dead, I'm sure he would not want you to act this way. You're not behaving as we must behave."

I was trying to help her, when suddenly the proprietor tapped at the door. It was another of Padre Pio's spiritual sons. Almost all of us were there [for the fiftieth anniversary of his reception of the stigmata]. He came up because he had heard the noise which we made. I opened the door and I saw him there. He said: "What can I do for you? What has happened? Can I do something for you?"

I said: "No, the Father is dead!"

I saw him grow white, white, really. His daughter was behind him. I shut the door suddenly because Giovanna was in a terrible state. I calmed her and said: "Giovanna, you must not behave like this, even if he is dead, even if it is a terrible thing. We must remember that from this moment on he will be judged on how we behave, and you cannot behave like that. He does not want you to be like that. You must be the serious woman of the Gospel."

She said: "Oh, yes, I know it, but please, for charity sake, go and see if it's true, because many times he had been very ill and then suddenly he was all right. Go and see if it's true."

I dressed quickly and went out. I rushed into the piazza. The first thing I saw was that there were already twenty carabinieri. They had never been there so early in the morning. It wasn't even three o'clock yet. It must have been around two thirty-five— around that time. I spoke to one of them who was standing in a long line with all the other carabinieri. I asked: "Can you tell me if it is true that the Padre, our Padre, is dead?"

He said: "I know nothing. I know nothing. I can know nothing till the sun comes up." That was the order he had had. The priests had called the carabinieri, because they knew that when the word of Padre Pio's death would become known, all the people would rush there. That was exactly what happened.

I went on, because I wanted someone to say that Padre Pio had died. Near the door of the church was the chief of the carabinieri—I don't know—maybe he was a soldier—something of that kind. I went near him and I said: "Please tell me! Is it true about Padre Pio?"

He said: "I know nothing. I don't know. I cannot speak until morning." That was all he said.

I said: "Please, do it! I ask you to do it for charity sake."

And he said: "*Look* at me!" So I looked at him. He was *weeping*. All his uniform . . . Then I went back.

About midday, after Padre Pio's body had already been exposed and we had seen him, the man who had come to tap on our door earlier came again. I said: "Please, I want to excuse myself. Please forgive me. I was in such a terrible state. Please forgive me. I know I ought not to have told you that, that way, abruptly: 'The Father is dead.' "

He said: "I was coming to thank you."

I said: "No, it was I who didn't realize . . . "

He interrupted. He said: "I was coming to thank you, because the shock . . . I had a great shock, but my daughter was there and she immediately gave me the medicine that I needed. After a short while I was well again. But if I had gone out and learned about it suddenly, I'd have fallen down dead."

So you see even in that, I cannot say that there was something extraordinary, but things happened in a way in which they didn't harm anyone. Nobody was hurt. Oh, it was a terrible night. Terrible. It was the most terrible night. I'll never forget it if I live for a hundred and fifty years.

5. Doctor Giuseppe Sala
San Giovanni Rotondo

Doctor Sala was Padre Pio's regular physician and attended him at the moment of his death. In my interview I did not seek a medical report. Sufficient clinical data exists, I believe, in Padre Pio's biographies, and in an entire book which Doctor Festa wrote specifically from his examinations of Padre Pio's stigmata: The Mystery of Science in the Light of Faith. *(Padre Pio joked: "It is better to be a mouse between two cats than Padre Pio between two doctors.") So in the few precious minutes I had with Doctor Sala, I sought mainly his comment on the psychological balance of Padre Pio, which is vital to a true understanding of the very validity of the stigmata. I am distressed by the appalling lack of professionalism of some journalists who, in their exposés of other stigmatics, have not given so much as a nod to the vast medical data that exists on Padre Pio. They simply lumped him summarily in their conclusion that his stigmata too were the result of hysteria.*

I began by inviting the doctor's opinion of an article in the January 1971 issue of the American Medical Association's journal that explained Padre Pio's stigmata as the result of hysteria and autosuggestion.—JS

* * *

The wounds were not at all the result of hysteria. That fact is certain. The stigmata existed independently of the character of Padre Pio, who was a gentle and calm person and not at all hysterical. Although there were scratches or marks on his face which he himself could have made, the stigmata were not self-made.

The stigmata were real wounds. They were not provoked or caused by irritation. They were outside of any physiopathological consideration. I don't know if hysteria is possible as a natural explanation of the stigmata—that because of hysteria a person could make himself appear to have holes in his hands and side.

[*I asked Doctor Sala's opinion of the medical reports of other doctors.*]

I am thinking of the report of Doctor Festa. Of the three doctors who examined Padre Pio's wounds, Doctor Festa was the most skeptical and critical, and his examinations and tests were severe. They were quite adequate, and I do not have anything to add to what he said. The report of Festa has detailed factual information on the circumstances of the wounds of Padre Pio. I could add comments as an observer of a greater person by a lesser, but in the long run my comments would be the same as those of Doctor Festa. The results are the same when they have the same objective.

When Padre Pio was ill, his blood showed the changes any normal person's would. There were no defects in his blood from the constant loss of blood. One might think that he would be anemic or without any blood. Absolutely not. In fact, it was normal.

His physiological manifestations were normal. The only thing that was beyond comprehension was the nature of the wounds. They were not inflamed or infected. They were normal wounds but not made by any type of instrument. They were a special type of wound in that they did not have the capacity to heal as normal wounds do. They had characteristics which, for a doctor, are important, because a doctor is interested in seeing if a wound is healing or if it is not going to heal. His wounds were beyond any anatomical classification. They were wounds that were unique—*sui generis.*

6. Doctors Pavone and Mazzoni
San Giovanni Rotondo

Doctors Pavone and Mazzoni are medical doctors on the staff of the Home for the Relief of Suffering.—JS

* * *

[*Doctor Mazzoni:*] Once I was talking with a professor from Florence whom Doctor Pavone was taking care of as a patient. When speaking of Padre Pio's stigmata, the professor said that they were probably the result of autosuggestion. Doctor Pavone told that to Padre Pio. Padre Pio laughed and told him to tell the good professor that he should think very intensely of an ox, and maybe he will be able to autosuggest himself into growing horns.

[*Doctor Pavone:*] Many times we came to see Padre Pio. We would spend a half hour or an hour. I approached Padre Pio as a medical man, with a well-trained, critical, analytical mind and spirit. Also keep in mind that I am a man of faith. There can be no adequate explanation of Padre Pio's personality—the person of Padre Pio—from a merely scientific viewpoint.

The problem with the stigmata is this: the wounds that Padre Pio had in his hands and feet and side never changed. They remained constant, probably from the day he got them and for the rest of his life, without any medication. The stigmata were real holes in the hands and feet, so that you could read a newspaper through the holes.

Every time I would see Padre Pio, I would approach him with the same critical analysis and skepticism that any doctor would have. However, many phenomena of Padre Pio were not explainable medically. We have clinical experience of things which we cannot explain.

There is also his charismatic dimension. Besides the stigmata, he had the crowning with thorns. He had the transverberation of his heart [Padre Pio's mystical experience, with intense physical pain, on August 5, 1918, of a sword being shafted through his heart, which occurred before he received the stigmata permanently on September 20, 1918]. He tried very hard to hide everything. About all his gifts he said, as Jesus said: "Don't tell anything about this to anyone."

[*I asked Doctor Pavone his opinion of Doctor Festa's book about Padre Pio's stigmata.*]

Truth has no age. Whatever was said thirty years ago cannot be witnessed today, but it is scientific truth. No one can contradict it. Doctor Festa was a Mason who became a convert to the Catholic Faith. His book shows that the stigmata, medically speaking, are a mystery. In their totality, they are a mystical phenomenon.

The early examinations of Padre Pio included sealing the wounds of his hands and side. After three days, their condition was identical to their previous condition. Vivid perfumed blood came out. Perfumed blood! When Padre Gemelli [a priest-psychologist very critical of Padre Pio's stigmata] read the book, he could not contradict it, because it was all true. In fact, he accepted it.

After the three medical examinations by Festa, Bignami and Romanelli, the medical case on Padre Pio was closed. These examinations were sufficient. Even the Church acknowledged the facts. Popes Pius XII and John XXIII accepted their authenticity.

[*I asked the doctors about Padre Pio's diet. Doctor Pavone responded.*]

He used to eat once a day. He ate very little. Little! He ate not little, but grams! He used to go once a day to the refectory [dining room] and only under obedience. He would make a joke out of it by putting some food on the plate of the person to his right and left. In the evening he would never go to the refectory.

In medical terms, Padre Pio's nourishment was absolutely insufficient. His diet was very skimpy. For him, one hundred calories a day were a lot—fifty to one hundred calories a day. He weighed about ninety kilograms [almost 200 pounds!]. On one occasion Padre Pio had a fever for four or five days. I myself witnessed this. He was sick and didn't touch anything except a drop of water. He presumed that he would lose weight. But after three days, when he weighed himself, he had gained four kilograms [almost nine pounds]. These things contradict human logic. They are against the natural law—against everything. But they happened.

Padre Pio was just skin and bones. When I touched his arm, it felt like the arm of a child. Sometimes when you tried to kiss his hand, it felt as if you were kissing the hand of a little child. Sometimes his hand seemed to be the hand of a giant. But his physical condition was irrelevant to him.

What was incredible was his lack of rest. [He slept for only an hour or two a night.] One day Padre Pio asked a young man how long he had slept the previous night. The man answered: "Six or seven hours."

Padre Pio said: "That's as much as I sleep in one year!"

All the pains and illnesses that came to Padre Pio, some of which were determined as bronchitis, and so forth, all were mysterious illnesses. I looked at him as a doctor. I couldn't give any explanation. There were illnesses that in the evening would become worse, and the temperature would go over 42 to 43 degrees centigrade [about 109 degrees fahrenheit]. It could break the thermometer.

At the Casa, Padre Pio taught us that medicine which is not fortified with the love of God is medicine that can never have any lasting results. Only science illumined by faith can have a lasting effect on a patient. He said: "Do everything out of love for Jesus Christ. Do it with love. Bring love." He continually told the nuns, the nurses, and the doctors: "When you see the patient, look at Jesus Christ. In every sick person, see Jesus suffering. In the poor whom you love, you see Jesus twice, because Jesus was very poor."

It is logical that the Casa, from its very inception, was defined as a temple of prayer and science. That is what Padre Pio wanted. From that union should arise science and faith. Often science seems to be the antithesis of faith, but true science cannot be opposed to faith, because there is no such thing as a double truth.

Truth is unique—it is only one. From the fusion of faith and science here in San Giovanni Rotondo you will be able to find the whole world in Jesus Christ.

7. Laurino Costa
San Giovanni Rotondo

Laurino is head chef at the Home for the Relief of Suffering. His traumatic encounter with Padre Pio (he saw blood streaming down the Padre's face!) is not typical in the sense that such an incident happened often. It is typical in the sense that almost anything could happen in the course of Padre Pio's ministry in the confessional. The interview begins with the strange sequence of events that brought Laurino to San Giovanni Rotondo.—JS

* * *

I had been living in a small town near Padua, and I was out of work. I heard about Padre Pio through a friend who used to come here. I myself had never met him. My friend gave me a small photograph of Padre Pio. It made a deep impression on me. I took it and put it in my pocket. Frequently at night I would dream of him.

Well, I thought, I might as well write to Padre Pio and ask for his blessing to help me find work. I sent Padre Pio a telegram. Immediately I received a telegram from him in in reply, telling me: "Come to San Giovanni Rotondo right away."

For me to go to San Giovanni Rotondo was no small thing. It was a long and expensive trip, and I was penniless at the time. But on February 4, 1958, I hitchhiked to Padua. At the train station I met a lady whom I knew and told her my story. A gentleman overheard our conversation and approached me. He said: "I am going to San Giovanni Rotondo by car. If you care to join me, you are welcome." I went along with him. My providential traveling companion was Doctor Gusso, a native of Padua, then the medical director of the Home for the Relief of Suffering.

I arrived at 4:00 a.m., in time to attend Padre Pio's Mass. After

Mass I went into the sacristy with all the other men to meet Padre Pio. The Padre beckoned to me with his hand. I did not budge. I thought he was looking for someone else. He called me out of the large crowd and said in a loud voice: "Laurino, come, come here!" He recognized me among so many people, although I had never seen him before and he had never seen me. I approached him, shaking like a leaf. He said: "Well, now, go and feed my sick."

I didn't know anything about cooking, and I had no intention to stay, but he insisted that I stay. I said: "But Padre, I'm not a cook. I have never cooked before. I don't know how to cook an egg."

Again he said: "Go and prepare the food for my sick."

I asked him: "Will you assist me? I've never been a cook."

He said to me: "Go. I'll be with you."

Someone showed me over to the hospital and introduced me to the mother superior. She greeted me with: "Oh, so you are the experienced cook we were expecting." I was too stunned to reply.

At 7:30 a.m. I went to the kitchen. It was a frightening sight— this great spacious kitchen with huge kettles, stoves, sinks, pipes, basins, kitchenware, and so forth. I never saw anything like that in my life. But the most alarming feature was the sight of the kitchen employees standing there, waiting for my orders.

However, as soon as I entered, I had the sensation that I had always been there. I felt as though being a cook had always been my trade. Everything seemed familiar to me. I had no doubt that I could do the cooking. So I went ahead with it. That first day I cooked for about 450 people.

After a short while Padre Pio wanted me to bring my family here. But I didn't want them to come. You see, in the northern part of Italy, in Padua, we are used to a different style of living. We think differently. We have different customs. When I first arrived here, I wanted to turn back immediately. I didn't like it at all here. However, Padre Pio insisted: "Let the family come here." So my family came and we settled down here. We have been here now for fourteen years.

Padre Pio never wanted me to leave. But after two or three years I had a few days off. I said: "Father, I want to go up north and see my mother and relatives."

He said: "Go, but come back immediately."

Again, just before he died, my days off were due, and I told him: "I'll go up north."

He said: "No!" But then he relented and said: "How many days do you intend to be away?"

I told him: "Father, about seven or eight days."

He said: "I will give you five days." That was precisely enough time to bring me back for Padre Pio's death.

When I first came here, I had some doubt in my mind that he was really a saint. Yes, I admitted, he might be a very special person, but a saint? I couldn't imagine Padre Pio as a saint. I never told anyone, even my wife, that I had such doubts. I kept them to myself.

Then one day I went to Confession to Padre Pio. I saw him in the confessional with his head tilted to one side, a deep cross on his forehead. His face was all bloody. He was staring at me, with his eyes fixed on me. *Mama mia!* I said to myself. I started to shake from fright. I called to him, but he didn't answer. He just stared at me, his eyes fixed on me. There was that blood running down from the cross on his forehead! I put my hand in my pocket. I wanted to get my handkerchief to wipe the blood off, but my hand remained in my pocket. I could not move. We just stared at each other for about ten minutes. I felt as if I were going to faint. I kept calling: "Padre! Padre!"

He then gave a big sigh. Still staring at me, *he* began to confess my sins. I didn't say a word. He told me all my sins—all the sins I was going to tell him. Then he gave me absolution. I still hadn't said anything, but he gave me absolution. Then he began to come to himself again.

He said: "Well, Laurino, how long ago was it that you made your last Confession?" I told him that it was nine days ago. He confessed my sins for the second time and gave me absolution for the second time. Then I saw that the blood began to disappear.

I got up very slowly. Then I saw that the cross had disappeared. I left the confessional. I let out a loud shriek—a very loud scream. There were a lot of other people in the sacristy who were waiting to go to Confession. They asked me: "What happened to you?" They thought that perhaps Padre Pio had chased me away. I began to cry. I went on crying for three days and three nights. I kept seeing him before my eyes as I had seen him in the confessional. I would go home at night but could not go to sleep until at least 2:00 or 2:30 in the morning. I said the rosary continuously. It went on and on like that.

I went to Padre Clemente and said: "Such and such happened to me. What should I do? Why did Padre Pio reveal himself like that to me?"

"Well, Laurino," Padre Clemente said, "ask him."

It's easy to say "Ask him," but I didn't have the courage to go into the church, because I kept seeing him like that. He was always before my eyes. I could not sleep. I could not eat. I wept continuously. I thought I was losing my mind. Really!

Then the head of the hospital told me to take hold of myself—that I had a family to think of. So one evening after work I was on my way home. I said to myself: I'll stop right now and see Padre Pio and ask him why he revealed himself to me like that.

I began to go up to the friary, but I couldn't make it. I lost courage. I couldn't go on. I turned around and began to go home. I got halfway home when I turned around. I forced myself to go back to the friary.

Finally I got as far as the end of the corridor. I saw Padre Pio leaning against the door outside his room as though he were waiting for me. As soon as I saw him, I gave out another loud scream. Again I turned around, but I was unable to move. I felt all knotted up inside and I was unable to utter a word.

He saw me and said: "Come, Laurino, come! What's the matter? What has happened to you?" But I just couldn't find my voice.

Finally I said: "Padre, tell me why you made me see you like that? Is it perhaps because of me that you suffer so much?"

"No," he replied. "You are such a fool. It was a grace that God wanted to give you."

You see, it happened because I didn't believe in his sanctity. After that experience, woe to anyone who would dare to touch him. I would have scratched his eyes out with my two fingers!

8. Giovanni Savino
San Giovanni Rotondo

I almost missed this interview, because of Giovanni's reluctance to talk about his miracle. I had heard that he had received a new right eye after dynamite exploded in his face and blew his eye out of its socket. Father Dominic Meyer, Padre Pio's secretary for twelve years, whose testimony is unimpeachable, had described the accident and the cure in a letter. But I wanted to get Giovanni's story firsthand. The day before I left Italy he reluctantly agreed to tell me what had happened. —JS

* * *

It was in February 1949. We were leveling the ground for the construction of an annex to the friary. The whole area was stony, and we had to blast away a tremendously big boulder.

Every morning when we would begin our work, I would first attend Mass. Then I would go along the corridor as far as the stairway to meet Padre Pio. I would kneel down and say: "Padre Pio, give me your blessing. I'm going to work." He would place his hands on my head.

On the morning of the twelfth he did something different. I said: "Padre Pio, give me your blessing."

He gave me a big hug and said: "Courage! I will pray to the Lord that you will not die." Those words upset me terribly—"I will pray to the Lord that you will not die." I started to cry. Padre Pio went upstairs.

For the next three mornings I knelt again for his blessing. Each morning he embraced me and repeated those same words. This happened on the morning of the thirteenth, the fourteenth, and the fifteenth.

On the fifteenth, another man and I went out to complete the job. At noon we ate our lunch and went back to work. Then toward two o'clock the accident happened.

We had set a charge of dynamite under the boulder and waited for a half hour, but the charge didn't go off. I went to take a look at it, and at that moment it exploded. Everything flew into the air. A piece of flying rock cut off a big branch of a nearby tree as if it were a twig. If that rock had hit me, it would have split me in two. The debris fell all over me. I blacked out. My whole face was burned. The skin of my whole face was raw.·

They rushed me to the hospital in Foggia, where the doctor treated my left eye. My right eye was gone. It had only raw flesh in the socket.

On the third morning the doctor came in. I heard him talk. I said to him: "Doctor, Padre Pio seems to be taking care of me. I don't want to make him sound silly, but I have been praying to him, and every day I could smell the aroma of his tobacco at my bedside." (Before I went to the hospital, I had told Padre Pio: "Send me a little tobacco before I leave, so that I will be able to smell your tobacco." But Padre Pio said: "No, I will not give it to you now, because I might get some of it in your eyes, and that would irritate them. That would blind you. When you come back, I'll give you a whole pack of tobacco.") Then the doctor began to treat my eyes.

After ten nights in the hospital in Foggia, one night around twelve-thirty or one o'clock, the two or three other men in my room were asleep. I could hear them breathing. I felt a gentle slap on my eye, on my right eye, which had been completely gone from its socket. I said: "Who touched me?" But no one was there. From that moment, I could see with my *right* eye—but not with my left eye! Again I smelled the aroma of Padre Pio's tobacco. It was a beautiful smell. It really seemed like a smell of heaven.

In the morning they brought me to be treated by the oculist. He unbandaged my head. My whole face had been bandaged. My face had all new skin. I said to the doctor: "I can see your hand."

He said: "Yes, turn this way. You could be using your left eye."

I said: "Yes, I can see with my right eye."

He said: "No, it is your left eye which you see with."

I said: "I can see with my right eye. I don't see anything out of my left eye."

He said: "Are you crazy? I'm telling you that you don't have a right eye any more. I'm treating only the left eye."

I said: "Doctor, I'm not crazy." I wanted to tell him: Maybe you are crazy. I said: "It is the right eye that I can see out of, not the left eye."

Then the doctor covered my left eye and said: "How many fingers am I holding up?"

"I said: "Five."

"And how many now?" I told him the correct number.

He looked into my eye, and he could see my eye. He said: "Well, now, who is the saint behind this?"

I said: "Padre Pio, and Our Lady of Grace" [the title of the friary and adjacent church].

He said: "Now I believe, too." He had been an atheist. He didn't understand anything. He didn't believe anything. He said: "Now I believe—I do believe, because this has happened right in front of me."

That summer Padre Raffaele wanted to send me to another oculist at the Polyclinic in Rome. I went to Padre Pio's room and said: "Padre, Padre Raffaele wants to send me to Rome. He says that there is a good doctor there for my left eye. I can't see out of it."

"No," he said, "we have the grace which we have asked for. We have already obtained it. Even if you go to Rome you will not get any better than you are right now."

Now I can't see out of my left eye. The doctor ruined it. Out of obedience I stayed in the hospital for thirty-one days. But they ruined my eye. I kept telling the doctor: "Doctor, don't put any medicine into my eye. I can't stand it any more. Only bring me some cold water, because there is nothing wrong with my eye. It is the medicine that's burning it."

They had put atropine in the eye. The front of my eye was swollen. I put an ice bag on it. Then I took it away and said: "Doctor, I will use this for my throat." It took ten days of suffering for me to get rid of the burning that the atropine had caused—to my left eye!

9. Padre Alberto, Capuchin
San Giovanni Rotondo

Padre Alberto knew Padre Pio as far back as their days together in the minor seminary at San Giovanni Rotondo when Padre Pio was his spiritual director. Madre Speranza, of whom Padre Alberto speaks, was born in Spain and was foundress of the Daughters of Divine Love, now an international religious community. Many people believe that she was a great mystic, with some kind of telepathic communication with Padre Pio. —JS

* * *

After Padre Pio's death I went to Collevalenza to give a conference on Padre Pio, and to learn about the work of Madre Speranza. She was a little nun. She held her rosary in her hands; her eyes were cast down. I said: "Madre Speranza, I am a Capuchin from San Giovanni Rotondo, and I have come here to give a conference on Padre Pio. Say a prayer for his beatification."

She answered me: "Yes, I always pray for that."

I asked: "Have you ever met Padre Pio?"

She said: "Yes, I have met him."

"When and where did you meet him?" I asked.

She answered: "In Rome."

I said: "Excuse me, Mother, but you are mistaken. Padre Pio never went to Rome. He was in Rome only once, in 1917, when he took his sister there when she was entering the convent. You were in Spain at that time."

Madre Speranza said: "No, Father. I met him when I was under investigation by the Holy Office" [now called the Congregation for the Doctrine of the Faith]. I think she told me it was 1939 or 1940, but I'm not sure of the date.

I said: "Noooo. Padre Pio never came to Rome. In 1939 or 1940? Never!"

She replied: "Yes, every morning for a year. I was going to the Holy Office, because I was under their investigation. Padre Pio used to come every day. He wore mittens. He blessed me, and I used to kiss his hands. That was in Rome, at the Holy Office."

I said: "It is impossible that Padre Pio was there."

She said: "I don't know, but Padre Pio was there."

I asked: "Are you sure it was Padre Pio?"

She said: "Surely, surely. I am certain that Padre Pio came."

I said: "Excuse me, Mother, but I can hardly believe what you tell me."

She said: "Father, I have no reason to lie. I met Padre Pio at the Holy Office. I prayed for him, and he promised to pray for me always."

I said: "What if you are deceiving yourself?"

She said: "No, I'm not deceiving myself. It really was Padre Pio."

I said: "Listen, Mother. If this is true, I'm glad, but do me a favor. Pray for Padre Pio."

She answered: "Yes, I've always prayed for Padre Pio, and I'll continue to pray for his beatification."

When I was talking with her, I insisted that I didn't believe her, but within myself I accepted what she said. She insisted that she had seen Padre Pio every morning, and she is a good nun. She prays a lot, just like Padre Pio. She isn't a person who makes up things. I drew the conclusion that Padre Pio had bilocated. You can write about this, because this is a true and beautiful story.

I remember Padre Pio before he received the stigmata [he received it visibly and permanently in 1918]. When we were kids, all of us used to call him "the holy friar." We used to say: "Let's go to Confession to the holy priest." The whole town used to call him the holy friar.

In 1917 he did not have the stigmata [visibly]. Later he was visited by the doctor of the hospital of Barletta [Doctor Romanelli], then by Doctor Festa. Previously Doctor Festa had been a Mason; he was converted to the Church. He wrote a book on the stigmata of Padre Pio to describe the cause of the wounds. Padre Pio was also examined by Doctor Bignami [an atheist].

All three doctors came to the consensus which other doctors had reached: the stigmata of Padre Pio were a phenomenon that science could not understand. The stigmata cannot be explained by natural causes. The three doctors excluded the possibility of Padre Pio having the stigmata as a result of hysteria. They said: "That is impossible."

Several times I saw the wounds through his feet, because I used to help him to wash his feet. I saw the wounds on the top and bottom of his feet, just as I frequently saw them on his hands when I kissed them. Our lips would kiss the crust of the wounds. He let us kiss them.

Also, Padre Pio kissed my hand three times. The first time was when I celebrated my First Mass. Another time I got very angry at him. I tried to kiss his hand, but he pulled it away. He said: "Go away." I resented that. I was near the window, along with Padre Ambrogio and Padre Cassiano. They were laughing. I said nastily: "What kind of a saint is that!"

I walked away and started down the stairs. Then Padre Pio put his hands on my shoulders. He turned me around. He took my hand and said: "Do you feel offended? I didn't mean it." Suddenly he took my hand and tried to kiss it. I pulled my hand away, but he said: "Let me kiss it."

I was confused. I said: "I'm not a Bishop."

But he insisted: "Give me your hand. It is the hand of a priest." And he kissed it.

[*As spiritual director, Padre Pio used to give conferences to the boys. I asked Padre Alberto about them.*]

In the little conferences which he gave us, he used to say: "Everything comes down to purity. Purity says it all." In particular, he had devotion to the Blessed Mother, and to Jesus in the Blessed Sacrament. He would instruct us of the depth, the grandeur, of our vocation. He would bring in examples from the life of St. Francis. Most of all he spoke about purity in connection with receiving Holy Communion. He suffered tremendously when he would see one of us receive Communion in sin.

He wanted us all to be Capuchins. He thought that was our

calling. He thought that every boy who came to the seminary had been called by God, and he insisted that they become Capuchins. Of course when they were not worthy of it, he suffered tremendously. For example, there were six of us boys in the seminary. Someone asked him: "Of the six, will all go to the novitiate? Will all of them be ordained priests?"

He became sad. He almost cried. He said: "No, only two." Now there are the two, who are stationed at San Giovanni Rotondo— Padre Christophero and myself. The others left.

[I asked Padre Alberto how Padre Pio might be relevant to people who have never met him.]

Let me tell you a story. Then you can draw your own conclusion. I was in San Severo. One day I accompanied Professor Maggio to San Giovanni Rotondo. His wife told me that he was an incredulous atheist. He didn't believe in anything—not in Padre Pio, not in an after-life. He came to San Giovanni Rotondo, and I presented him to Padre Pio in the corridor. It was afternoon, and Padre Pio was coming out of his room.

This man, a professor, when he saw Padre Pio, trembled. He was speechless. Padre Pio drew near him. I said: "Padre Spirituale, this is Professor Maggio. He has come here from San Severo. He is an invalid from the war." The professor didn't say a word.

Padre Pio asked him: "Where were you wounded?"

Nothing! Maggio didn't say a word.

Padre Pio asked him again: "Where were you wounded?"

Nothing! He didn't answer.

I was quite surprised. I thought: What's happening? Why doesn't he answer? Finally I said: "Padre Pio, please pray for him and his family—for a particular intention, and give him a special blessing." Padre Pio blessed him and wished him well and said goodbye to him affably.

When we were outside, I said: "Professor, you didn't say a word. What kind of an impression did you get?"

He said: "Padre Alberto, Padre Pio isn't a man." I asked him what he meant.

He said: "He is a supernatural being. He is a man of another world. As soon as I saw him, he impressed me. I felt a choking in my throat. I wanted to say a few words, but nothing could come out. You know—Padre Pio is an angel!"

A lot of people have had that same impression. For many, Padre Pio is a myth. He is a supernatural being. He is like Christ reincarnated. So many people tell me that—he is like a reincarnated apostle sent by God to stem the evil of people, and to lead souls along their way to Christ. For these people, Padre Pio is already a saint. For the rest, people who have never met or heard of him, you are the one to tell them about him.

[*As a conclusion to this interview, I would like to quote from an article by Padre Alberto, written in the* Voice of Padre Pio, *describing how he witnessed a case of bilocation of Padre Pio. This is what he wrote.*]

One afternoon in May 1928, I was going from the chapel toward the stairs. As I neared the window which opens onto the cloister, I saw Padre Pio near the window, staring out, his gaze fixed toward the mountain. He seemed absorbed. I drew near to kiss his hand, but I had the sensation that his hand was stiff. At the same moment I heard him pronounce the words of absolution in a very clear voice: "I—I—absolve—you—you—from your sins." His voice had the same effort to pronounce the words which was characteristic of him giving absolution.

Immediately I ran to call the Father Tomaso, the superior. The two of us approached Padre Pio, who was pronouncing the last words of absolution. At that Padre Pio gave a jerk as if he had come back out of drowsiness. He turned to us and said: "You are here? I didn't realize you were here."

A few days later a telegram arrived at the friary from a city in northern Italy. The telegram thanked Father Superior for having sent Padre Pio to assist a dying man. From the telegram we understood that the man was dying at the exact moment Padre Pio was pronouncing the words of absolution.

10.　Andre Mandato
North Plainfield, New Jersey

*Not everyone coming to Confession to Padre Pio was a Prodigal Son.
Many were like the Prodigal Son's brother: they had never left their
father's home, but they still needed a word of admonition. Day by day
Padre Pio used the forum of the confessional to cultivate in them a sense
of sin—a sense of the malice of venial sin. Sometimes his therapy with
his penitents was traumatic, as described briefly but vividly by Andre
Mandato. His son, Pio Mandato, has recently been ordained as a
Capuchin priest in the New Jersey Capuchin Province of the Stigmata.
—JS*

*　*　*

I had been going to church every Sunday but I had no strong
belief in Confession. I went very seldom. I started to believe in
Confession only after I went to Padre Pio.

The first time I confessed to him, he told *me* what sins I had
committed. He told me: "You swear."

I said: "Yes, Father."

"Then you ask God to forgive you. That's not enough," he said.

This shocked me. As soon as I left the confessional (and this I
can't forget as long as I live) I felt inside of myself something
crushing me. I started to cry, cry—I couldn't hold my tears. For
the first time I really understood what it means to offend God. I
do not swear anymore. This is a grace I got from Padre Pio. Never
again will I sin and then close my eyes and do nothing more than
say: "God forgives me."

Priests today give you a penance of a Hail Mary or an Our
Father. Padre Pio would make you do penance for thirty days!
The sins I confessed weren't big, but he gave me one month! It
was a good lesson for me not to offend God anymore. That was
his purpose—to make me understand.

I first visited Padre Pio when I was eighteen or nineteen, along with my friend. He impressed us. My friend said to him: "I don't believe in God. I'm not sure that there is a God."

Padre Pio looked at him and said: "You're crazy."

At that time there wasn't much of a crowd, because it was hard for the people to get there. We could go into the little garden, where there were maybe ten people, and we visited with him. He was jovial, in good humor. He told jokes. When you were by yourself you would say: He is a saint. But when he talked with you, you didn't see the saint. You saw a human being like everybody else, smiling, joking. I could touch him. I'd talk with him just as I talk with you.

I had been a tailor in Bologna. In 1961 I decided to come to the United States, and Padre Pio helped me. One night I dreamed of him. With great clarity he made me understand that my application for admission to the United States had been rejected. I told him that it meant a lot to me to come, and he told me to try again—that I should submit my petition again with a new sponsor and that all would go well.

When I awoke, I did not know whether or not to believe this dream. But the suspense was not long. That afternoon I learned that my request to emigrate had been rejected. Soon afterwards I applied again and was given a visa for myself and all my family.

[*I asked Mr. Mandato if he recalled any anecdotes for which Padre Pio was famous.*]

Here is one of the stories I remember. A lawyer died and went to heaven. But he got tired, because after two months he didn't have any cases. Then one day he came up with a case. He said: "I don't think Saint Peter should have the keys of heaven." Someone asked him why.

The lawyer answered: "Saint John the Baptist should have Saint Peter's job. Saint John was the cousin of Jesus. He was Jesus' precursor. He has the right to the keys of heaven."

Everybody began to agree with the lawyer. The talk about this went all over heaven. The heavenly Father heard the commotion and said: "What's going on here?" They told him the story. He said: "Let's take it to court."

Saint Peter stood there with the keys in his hand, and the lawyer was on the other side. The Father said to the lawyer: "What do you have to say?"

The lawyer answered: "Almighty Father, excuse me, but I think that Peter should not have the keys." The Father asked why.

The lawyer said: "Saint John the Baptist is the cousin of Jesus, your own Son. John was his precursor, the one to talk about Jesus' coming." His words were eloquent.

The Father nodded as if to say yes. Saint Peter got scared. He thought: I'm going to lose my keys. The keys dropped from his hands onto the ground.

Then the Father said to the lawyer: "What you said sounds right, but that is not what my Son did. What He did stands forever."

Then Saint Peter picked up his keys and said to the lawyer: "You are the last lawyer to come to heaven. After this, no more lawyers get in!"

In San Giovanni Rotondo, Padre Pio made all people equal. The rich became poor, the poor became rich. That is San Giovanni Rotondo, where you can talk from your heart. You can share your problems with somebody else. Nobody boasts: "I am so-and-so." No! Everybody says: "I am a poor man, too, in search of peace."

11. Padre Alessio, Capuchin
San Giovanni Rotondo

If a Capuchin is seen in a photograph of Padre Pio, very likely it is Padre Alessio. He had the unique and awesome privilege of attending Padre Pio for the last three years of Padre Pio's life, when Padre Pio was almost completely incapacitated by illness. He is the English correspondent for the Capuchins in San Giovanni Rotondo. I began my interview by asking him if there had been any decline in the number of pilgrims coming to San Giovanni Rotondo after Padre Pio's death.—JS

* * *

Exactly the contrary is true. The number of people coming here is increasing. All the hotels which were small before his death are building larger accommodations. The only difference is that while Padre Pio was alive, people would stay here for five or ten days, even a month; but now they stay for only a few days. The number of pilgrims is increasing, especially on Sundays. Last month, for example, we had between seven and ten thousand people here. Last May we had about fifty buses every Sunday.

We receive about seventy letters a day from the English-speaking world. That includes letters from the United States, England, Ireland, Sri Lanka (Ceylon), Pakistan, Canada, the Philippines, Kuwait, Australia, Burma, even China. I don't know what the total volume of mail is, but I believe that mail from Italy is less than from English-speaking countries.

[*I asked Padre Alessio to outline a typical day in Padre Pio's life.*]

Ordinarily Padre Pio offered daily Mass at 4:00 a.m. This was for most of his life, until close to the end. Toward the end we generally encouraged him to offer Mass at 4:30 or 5:00, but we didn't succeed in this. For a while he said Mass at 5:00 a.m., but then it was changed back to 4:00. We had to keep the church doors closed until five minutes before his Mass. If we had opened them earlier, he would want to begin immediately. If we had opened the church at 3:30, he would want to say Mass then. As soon as we opened the church, he was trying to go to the altar. It was as if something was trying to move him to say Mass.

For breakfast he would have a cup of coffee, but he never finished it. Sometimes we tried to have him take an egg, but it was hard to convince him to eat it. That was in 1965.

Here we have the custom of "first fruits." Whenever we had the first fruits, the new fruits of the season, he would never touch them. He never ate anything at all on the feasts of St. Michael, St. Francis, the Immaculate Conception, and the other feasts of Our Lord and Our Lady. He began to give up *everything* a few days before these feasts. These were his acts of mortification—having something which he could eat, and wished to eat, but he set it aside. Generally whenever he ate anything, he would eat very little, but when we had those feasts, he didn't touch anything at all.

Sometimes we would put a plate of macaroni in front of him. He would nibble at it and say: "Oh, I'm full. I'm bursting." I'd eat an egg and try to get him to eat one. He would say: "No." It would have been absolutely impossible for us to live for a week the way he ate.

His diet had no protein. After the doctors examined him, they instructed him to eat peas, which have a lot of protein. They were distasteful. He ate only a few spoonfuls to please the doctors. For lunch we would bring him a lot of dishes, but he would hardly touch them.

During the day, if Padre Pio was working at his desk, he would have a glass of water, or a cup of coffee or anise, or perhaps a glass of wine or vermouth, but even in these little things he would deny himself. He liked them, but he would only touch them to his lips. His whole life was an act of mortification, suffering.

[*I asked Padre Alessio to describe the stigmata.*]

I saw for myself early in 1968 that the wounds were very deep. I didn't see any light through the stigmata, because the top and bottom were crusted with blood. But if the top and bottom of the hands were clean, it is true that you could see through them. The wounds went completely through. The only thing that prevented this from being seen was the blood which was coagulated on the palms of his hands.

When I took care of Padre Pio, I would wash his face but not his wounds. He did that himself, except toward the end of his life, when Padre Onorato helped him wash his wounds. But I did see the wounds when I was in his room.

One day after he had gone to bed he didn't call me. He used to call me back into his room after about eight or ten minutes, but this day I didn't hear his bell ring. I let two or three minutes pass and went into his room. It was about fifteen minutes after he had gone to bed. I was scared, because something so different was happening. I knocked on the door and said: "May I come in?"

He said: "Come in, my son, and help me."

I found him half on the bed and half on the floor. I don't know what happened. At the time he had been very sick. Perhaps he had tried to get up and became faint. The gloves [fingerless mittens which he wore all day except at Mass] were on the floor. I immediately lifted him up onto the bed. Then he sat down on the bed. I saw the wounds and cleaned them, using what was there.

The wounds were about as big as a penny. They were very deep. They were covered with half-coagulated blood. I cleaned the blood very hurriedly. I was very afraid every time I touched them. The wounds on the palms of the hands were closed up by the dried blood but the backs of his hands were all bloody, so I cleaned them.

I saw the wound in his side, but only the horizontal wound. I didn't see any vertical wound which would form a cross. The wound was almost three inches long and a quarter inch wide. It was under his left breast.

Generally Padre Pio changed the gloves every two to three days, depending on the amount of blood that was coming out. Before Mass, when Padre Pio would pull off his mittens in the sacristy, scabs of blood would sprinkle down on the vesting table, and people would take them. I have one of these scabs which is over an eighth of an inch thick.

The stigmata bled continuously. Sometimes when the friars would remove the sheets from his bed, they were filled with blood. Padre Pio wrote to his spiritual director, who put him under obedience to describe the stigmata, that if God hadn't sustained him when he received them, he would have died.

The stigmata were also very painful. People used to grasp his hands roughly, and he would shout at them. That offended them. One person said: "What did I do to you?" He answered: "Do you think they are decorations?" He feared so much for his hands and his feet. If he knew that someone was going to kiss his hands, he would immediately keep his hands close to himself. One day a woman knelt down and touched his foot. My goodness! The shout he let out! He shouted so loud! Then we helped him to continue to walk, but he was limping.

[*I asked Padre Alessio about Padre Pio's assaults by the devil.*]

When he was a young man, people living with him in the friary could hear him fighting with the devil, or they would hear the noise of chains. While I was taking care of him as an old man, there was an intercom in his room, which we always kept turned on. My room was very close to his, and I could hear everything, even his breathing, so he was never really alone—I could hear every word. I looked after him day and night, but I had to try to get some sleep at night to be able to help him during the day.

One night when he was seventy-eight years old, he called me every five or ten minutes. I got a bit upset. I said to him: "Why do you keep asking me to come, and then when I do, you don't have anything to say to me?" He would be in bed saying his rosary. I got angry, and I said to him: "Why are you calling? You know that I must look after you tomorrow, and I must get at least a few hours of sleep."

He just said: "My son, stay in this chair and sleep here. Stay here, because they don't leave me alone. They don't give me even a minute's sleep." By "them" he meant the devils. The devils were around him like beasts, trying to disturb his prayers or his meditation. My presence would save him from something or someone. I don't know from whom, but I'm sure they weren't the angels.

[*I asked Padre Alessio if Padre Pio feared going to hell.*]

One day the mountain behind us was all on fire. There was smoke all over the place. He said: "My goodness! I never slept a minute last night, because I was thinking of hell," but I have never heard him express any fear of going to hell.

[*I asked if Padre Pio had spoken favorably about the alleged apparition of the Blessed Virgin at Garabandal.*]

About Garabandal he said: "I don't know anything. The Church must decide about the apparitions and all those things." He didn't want to anticipate the judgment of the bishops and the Church.

[*Many people speak about Padre Pio's gruffness with them. I asked Padre Alessio for a comment.*]

One day I was with Padre Pio in the room near the sacristy. It was jam-packed, and we couldn't get through with the wheelchair. I was alone with him and with Brother Bill Martin [now an ordained Capuchin, Father Joseph Pius], trying to push our way through the crowd. We were shouting: "Let him get through," but we couldn't get through. The people would not cooperate.

Padre Pio too was shouting: "Let me through!"

I had to tell the people: "Don't let him get angry or upset."

Finally when we did get through the crowd, he said: "Don't worry. I didn't get angry in my soul. I was shouting, but my heart was laughing."

The only time some people respected him was when he shouted at them. He told me: "I'll never get angry inside myself. If I ever get angry inside, it won't be for this reason."

The same applies to his roughness in the confessional—it was only to make people live a good life. His harsh words, his shouting, were something that changed people. They would tell me that they had been away from God for forty, fifty, or sixty years. When Padre Pio shouted at them, it was the shock or jolt they needed to come back to God.

[*I asked Padre Alessio: Surely there must have been some who refused his help and resented his rough treatment.*]

No, there was no one. Perhaps in some cases there was resentment as an immediate reaction. Padre Pio might say: "Go away, go away from me and come back here in two months." Then after two months they were back, and he accepted them and gave them absolution.

[*I asked how Padre Pio would guide people as their spiritual director.*]

He would insist on their participating daily in the sacrifice of the Mass and Holy Communion. Also, for people who were advanced in the spiritual life, he would counsel a half hour of meditation or contemplation on the mysteries of our faith, especially on the Eucharist.

It was to promote this idea that he began the Prayer Groups. Another reason for the Prayer Groups was to have his spiritual children pray for his intentions and especially the intention of the Pope. He said that if they would do this, they would advance in the spiritual life. He said that if they would pray for a half hour, they would need more than a half hour of meditation. By following this guidance, the people were led to attend more than one Mass. You can see these same people in church today. They will come running, scampering up the hill to the church whenever Mass is offered. They are all his spiritual children. They know the importance of this mystery.

[*I asked Padre Alessio to describe Padre Pio's personality—was he a good conversationalist?*]

That depends on what time of the day you are referring to. Every day after Benediction he would go to the garden with his friends and confreres. All of us would sit there and listen to him. He was the only one who would do the talking—telling funny stories and things that happened to him or to his friends. It was the same in the refectory [dining room]. He usually carried the whole conversation. We really enjoyed listening to him. If someone had had a bad day, Padre Pio would have a special joke for his benefit, but he always knew how to avoid offending the other party. Sometimes he would say only a few words. He knew exactly what to say.

Sometimes we would visit Padre Pio in his room. He was a good conversationalist there, too. I was close to Padre Pio when he was old and sick—for about the last two or three years of his life. When people would come into his room, he would listen to them for a few minutes. Then if they were only chatting, he would say: "Okay, stop." He would listen to them for a while, but he would not continue to listen to idle chatter. Remember that he was very tired and always in great pain. It was extremely difficult for him to breathe. Especially during the winter he would get asthma attacks. The only consolation he experienced was saying his rosary. He prayed it night and day. He would rather do that than let a person continue with a lot of small talk.

[*I asked Padre Alessio if he had ever spoken to Padre Pio about bilocation.*]

No, and I don't know that he ever spoke about it. One day I was in his room. He was in bed, and I was sitting in the armchair. Both of us were fully awake. I could hear him praying the rosary. I too was praying the rosary. Then all of a sudden he stopped, and I heard him say: "Come here! What do you want?"

Again after a few seconds he said: "Come here! What do you want?" then with a more insistent tone he said again: "Come here! What do you want?"

Then I heard him pronounce the words of absolution for Confession: "Ego te absolvo . . . I absolve you . . . and for your penance you will say five Our Fathers and five Hail Marys and five Glory to the Fathers." Then he was silent.

Another day I asked him if he would ever go to Lourdes. He said: "I don't have to go to Lourdes. I go there every night. I see Our Lady of Lourdes every night." They are his own words.

[*I asked Padre Alessio about a phenomenon frequently associated with Padre Pio—various aromas experienced by people all over the world. There must be a basis of truth to many of their claims.*]

When people received these aromas, they would try to explain them. Someone would smell roses and then receive a grace. Someone would smell incense and be inclined to pray. Every day I heard these things, but how could I prove anything? There is consistency in their stories. They smelled something, and they would receive a favor from Padre Pio. If they would smell something that wasn't nice, then something tragic would happen, like a car crash or a broken leg.

12. Father Joseph Pius, Capuchin
San Giovanni Rotondo

Many visitors to San Giovanni Rotondo have come to know Father Joseph Pius Martin. They might have met this Brooklyn-born young man before Padre Pio's death, when he was known as Brother Bill Martin. After Padre Pio's death he was ordained as a Capuchin priest and is now known either as Father Bill Martin or by his religious name: Father Joseph Pius. He visited Padre Pio out of curiosity, and then he returned to stay. Few Capuchins (perhaps none) were closer to Padre Pio. His main task was to take personal care of Padre Pio. I began this precious interview by asking him about his background.—JS

* * *

I lived in Flatbush when I first heard about Padre Pio from a seminarian friend. That led me to visit Padre Pio for the first time in 1959. I came just as a tourist who was attracted to him because I had heard about him, like a person would visit the Eifel Tower because he had heard about it.

Then in 1964 I visited Padre Pio again and decided to stay for a while. Three times I was ready to leave, but he stopped me. He said: "No, you have to stay here." One of these times my bag was packed for me to go home the next day, but I stayed.

Padre Pio was guiding me at this time when I didn't even have a chance of becoming a religious. He accepted me as a spiritual son. By this I understood that he would pray for me. But for him it evidently meant a great deal more. Because he became my Spiritual Father, my life had been set along a path which was still open to me but which I could not yet see.

For the first year and a half I remained as a layman outside of the friary, and for three years I was a Third Order Brother living in the friary. After Padre Pio died, I applied for admission as a Capuchin priest in this Province (the Province of Foggia). I completed the required seminary formation and was ordained a priest.

The whole length of the Viale Cappuccini [the town's main thoroughfare] is filled with people who have come here from all over the world, from Italy, Switzerland, Germany, South America, North America, Tunisia in North Africa, Canada. The greatest influx began after World War II. For five years before his death, from 1963 to 1968, at least one hundred people came to San Giovanni Rotondo to stay.

[Padre Pio's intense sufferings were always for a purpose: to bring the grace of God down on others. I asked Father Joseph Pius if Padre Pio ever philosophized on the value of suffering.]

I never heard him philosophize about suffering. I remember hearing something he said or wrote: "Souls have a great price, and we have to buy them as Christ did." That was the idea. His vocation was to suffer for the redemption of mankind. Christ chose to suffer, and for that reason it has great value. Padre Pio chose to suffer along with Christ.

You will find Padre Pio the theologian, the philosopher, in the Passion of Christ, because Padre Pio was a living crucifix for fifty-eight years. I don't know if Padre Pio ever made any statements on suffering. I have never heard any, other than in the last few years of his life. He once said: "The person who is sick is celebrating Mass." That's a pretty strong statement.

[I asked if he had ever seen Padre Pio's stigmata.]

Yes, I saw the wounds in his hands and his side. The wounds in his hands—everyone who attended his Mass saw the stigmata, because when he held up his hands they were all bloody. His sleeves would pull back a bit and you would see that the entire area covered by the mittens was clotted with blood, with dried scabs of blood. The blood was always running out of the wounds, out of the holes. It would coagulate on the palms and the upper part of his hands so that it seemed that the stigmata covered the whole hand. They didn't. The actual wounds were in the center of the palms, and the coagulated blood covered the whole hand.

It is true that if you were very close and there was a light behind his hand, you could see a light shining through the holes in his hands. I myself never did see a light shine through them, because at Mass I was not that close to him. However, I did see the wounds at Mass. Mrs. Emilia Sanguinetti, the widow of the doctor who helped Padre Pio found the hospital, said that when Padre Pio celebrated Mass at St. Anthony's altar years ago and held up his hands to bless the people, she would see the light through his hands.

Padre Pio himself washed his wounds in the privacy of his room with spirits of camphor. He washed his own hands and his side, and Father Onorato washed his feet. I saw the wounds of his hands and side, but I never saw the wounds in his feet. His feet—they were always swollen—very swollen. They were like melons under his socks, one more swollen than the other.

In the last few months of his life, his wounds were not as bloody. Previously, he would take his gloves off before Mass, and crusts of blood would fall on the vesting table. As he approached the end of his life, they were not as bloody. It was more a serum that came out. He stopped cleaning his wounds about two months before he died.

Exactly when the stigmata were closed, I don't know. They had closed before he died. And when he died there was no scar, as is proven in the photographs that were taken within an hour after his death. He died without blood.

On the last day I did find white, pink crusts, or dried skin. During his last Mass, on the morning of September 22, I took away some of those crusts as he went out to say Mass. There was a tone of pink in them, very pale pink.

I like the reason Padre Odorico gave for the disappearance of Padre Pio's stigmata: "The signs of the stigmata were to help the priesthood of Padre Pio. The priesthood was finished, so the signs were finished."

[*I asked Father Bill about the aromas so frequently associated with Padre Pio.*]

A pleasant scent, such as from a rose, probably means that a grace or a favor has been granted or will be granted. Tobacco means danger. An acidy or medicinal smell means mortification or penance. Incense means prayer. I saw a list of fourteen smells! I don't hold to it. I think that list is fanatical.

[*I asked his opinion on Barbara Hildenbrand's article in the American Medical Association journal, concluding that Padre Pio's stigmata were the result of hysteria—mind over matter.*]

Read Father Carty's pamphlet *Science and the Stigmata*. It makes it very clear that hysteria cannot produce the stigmata. Hysteria can cause marks or blotches, but hysteria cannot give the actual stigmata. If the cause was hysteria, how is it that in fifty years they didn't become gangrenous?

Padre Pio was not even emotional. Never once did I see him approach an emotional state which could even get him on the road to hysteria. I saw him at the worst period of his life. In the last three years of his life he was suffering in soul and body in a way that was nothing less than horrible. We can never understand what that state was like for him. So if at any time he would have been emotional or hysterical, it would have been during this time. That never occurred.

Just think of him having open bleeding wounds on his body which were always there, every day, plus the fact that he suffered the flagellation [the scourging], the carrying of the cross, the crowning with thorns—the entire Passion. When I have a headache, I'm a little grumpy. But think of that man, who was always calm.

I'm not trying to cover up anything. He was Italian, but he was not what I can really call emotional. At the same time I don't want to give you the impression that he was sedate in his character. No. He was *vivace*, as they say, but not at all emotional or hysterical.

[*Padre Pio frequently longed to die. I asked Father Joseph Pius's comment.*]

Yes, he wanted to die, and understandably. But he was never morbid about it. He would say: "I'm tired, and I want to die." He prayed the rosary-novena to Our Lady of Pompeii for the grace to die. He just wanted to be with God and nothing in this world could possibly interest him. I've often wondered if Our Lady hadn't given him such an extraordinary charitable work as the Home for the Relief of Suffering to give him an interest in *something* on this earth.

Once I heard that Padre Sexto said to him on the occasion of an anniversary: "I wish you another fifty years."

Padre Pio answered him: "What harm have I ever done to you?"

When I would ask him how he felt, without putting on a long face he would say: "The cemetery is the only thing that is left," or "The tomb is the only thing that remains."

He had forecast his own death by nine years. One day Padre Romolo asked him: "Padre Pio, are you afraid of death?"

He thought for a minute and then said almost flippantly: "No." Of course for Padre Pio death was his real goal in life. It is for everyone, but we don't feel it as strongly as he did.

The Friday before Padre Pio's death was the fiftieth anniversary of the stigmata. Padre Carmelo, the superior, came into his room and knelt down by the armchair and said: "Padre Pio, congratulations!"

Padre Pio answered him: "Why?" Certainly he realized that it was the fiftieth anniversary of his receiving the stigmata.

Padre Carmelo said: "Well, for fifty years of trouble."

Padre Pio corrected him: "Oh, but it is fifty-eight years." I heard him with my own ears. He was referring to the first time he received the stigmata in September 1910. Those wounds didn't remain [that is, they did not remain visibly between 1910 and 1918], but the pain did.

In spite of all this, Padre Pio had a sense of humor. Not only a sense of humor, but a very refined sense of humor that I would call wit. He was jovial. He was always joking without being silly— he was never silly. I think his sense of humor was God-given. The man suffered so much that if he didn't have a sense of humor he would have been a manic depressive. Not only did he have great physical and moral sufferings for his entire life, but he was always hearing the troubles of other people. I think Our Lord purposely gave him this wonderful sense of humor. Padre Pio would tell jokes and funny stories and entertain people during the recreation period. He would be the life of the party.

There are so many of those tiny little stories. You would go in and say: "How are you?" He would answer: "I'm sitting down."

He would take little things and build them up into big jokes, for example the story about a man from the back woods who wanted to take ride on the train. He went into the train station, and they asked him: "Don't you want a ticket?"

The man said: "Well, yeah, if I need one."

"Where are you going?"

"What importance is it to you where I'm going?"

This would go on and on and on. Finally the man bought a round trip ticket. They went into a dark tunnel. He got terribly scared. He asked: "Where are we going?"

His companion answered: "We are going into hell."

The man said: "Don't worry. I got round trip tickets."

Padre Pio would build it up. He was a comic when he wanted to be, without ever being silly and without ever losing a sense of the seriousness of his real work inside and outside of the confessional.

One day a woman visited him who was rather plump and all done up in ruffles and perfume and flowers. She came to him and said: "Padre, today I am sixty. Say something nice."

He leaned over and said: "Death is near!"

Things like that would floor me. They are endless. Plus the fact that in the last three years of his life he had gone into a bad period. He was starting to close in and just pray. He would repulse everything. As a matter of fact, I remember about a year before he died, the superior, Padre Carmelo, (Lord rest him) went in and said: "Padre, you don't smile anymore."

I can't give you a catalog of his jokes and witticisms, but he was terrific. Whether he was serious, solemn, or joking, he had a special command of the language that was all his own. He would slip in some dialect when he knew that people would understand him. It was great!

[*Nevertheless, Padre Pio could treat people quite roughly. I invited Father Joseph Pius's comment.*]

Oh, indeed! Padre Pio could be quite severe if he wanted to be. But you must remember what was happening. First of all, I never saw any instance when he was severe with anyone in front of other people. If he would be severe with anyone in public, those cases would be very rare, and he would act that way only if he didn't have the chance to confess that person.

I once heard that someone came into the sacristy who had come to San Giovanni Rotondo with his wife. He had the intention of killing her. He was planning a phony car accident on the curving road that goes down the mountain. When he came into the sacristy, Padre Pio suddenly turned around and said: "Murderer!" Pointing right at him, he said: "What are you doing here?" That was the moment of truth for the man. He repented. [Apparently it was this same incident that was described by an eyewitness in an article in *Sign Magazine*, February 1969, page 27, "Memories of Padre Pio." The author, Joseph Tusiani, said: "I was too young to understand the full impact of those words. I only recall the fury in his eyes."]

Remember what his real work was: he was a surgeon of the soul, and his real work was done in the confessional. If a person was not prepared, he would send that person away. He would do that frequently. However, he was a very old man who excelled in the virtues of patience and charity. He asked Our Lord: "How can I reach these souls? How can I make an impression on them? How can I really get to them, to crack through that exterior, that facade which they have built up through their egotism?" At least that is my interpretation of the way he acted.

Not everyone understood this. He would give them a shock by sending them away, even by yelling at them. But his only purpose was the same as that of Doctor Barnard, who would give a shock to a new heart to get it going. Padre Pio knew very well that if he just let people come in and confess and sent them away, they would not remodel their lives or renew their lives. But if he gave them that shock—and to be refused by him was really a shock, because nobody's ego is prepared to be sent away—they would always go to another priest and confess, or they would return to Padre Pio. That was what happened. They did change their lives.

I remember so very well just a few weeks before he died, Padre Onorato and I were at the men's confessional. We were leading Padre Pio past a line of people, when suddenly Padre Pio let go in front of a man. I tell you, I wanted to go and crawl into a corner. We got into the elevator, and the minute the door closed, Padre Onorato said: "Padre Spirituale," as they called him in the friary, "you can't do these things. You can't treat people like that. You will offend them."

Padre Pio very calmly, with a smile on his face, said: "But I want to offend them." For me, that was a key. I will grant that there might have been a slight defect in his character, but if there was, I personally think he overcame it.

It was interesting to see him go down a line of people. To one person he would give his hand to be kissed; another person he would tap on the head; another person he would ignore; another person he would *yell* at, to the point sometimes that people who were with him—I myself—would be embarrassed at his actions in front of the people.

Remember that he dared not be very sweet with people, because as it was, they would come with scissors and cut his habit or his cord or his vestments. He could never wear a skull cap as the friars do in Italy, because they would steal it from him. If he had been sweet and mild with people, they would have eaten him alive—that's what Padre Alessandro said, and it's true. You laugh, but think of poor Padre Pio. He had to go through that every day.

Finally, remember that when he acted gruffly with certain people, it was done with a supernatural intention. His interior, his soul, was never disturbed. I call him an actor for souls. It was done only with permission of the Lord. To get at their souls he would use a rough voice and be harsh with them. Then when he would leave the room, he would suddenly turn and say pleasantly: "Goodnight, everyone," very sweetly and calmly.

So it was actually a gift that Padre Pio had—to know how to act toward each individual person. We call it the "reading of souls." I saw it for myself. One day I went to Confession to him. When I finished, he said: "Well, what else?"

I said: "Nothing." It wasn't that I was trying to conceal a sin. I wasn't even conscious of a sin. But he said that to point out to me the need to increase the practice of a certain virtue. I wasn't even thinking of it. Since then I have been trying, really. He showed me a defect which I had to overcome.

There are other stories of his knowledge of a soul, and of the future. During the war he would tell people where they could find relatives, giving them the exact address. Accounts like that are endless. People would ask if they should have an operation or not. One doctor might say yes, another would say no. Padre Pio might, for example, say it's better to have it, and events would prove him right.

One time a lady came to him who is a telephone operator in Perugia. She had a choice of jobs between television and the telephone company. She could have received double her present salary if she had chosen a TV career. But Padre Pio said: "Tell her that it is better to eat onions and bread than to lose her soul. Tell her to work for the telephone company." He could see the whole future. He could see that the choice would be either good or bad for the person.

There is no end to these stories. I could talk till doomsday about them. Think of his fifty years of public life—365 days of the year—with people asking him questions and getting answers. There was no end to it.

A lady from Perugia went to Padre Pio because her son had married, but the couple were unable to have children. They began to bicker with one another: "It's your fault. No, it's your fault! Why did we get married?" And so forth. So the fellow's mother went to Padre Pio and kept repeating the story to him. Finally he said to her: "Be quiet!" Some time after that, two sons were born.

Sometimes his gift of knowledge helped him to hear

Confessions. He spoke English to me one day! He spoke English to Victor Kelly, of New York, while Victor was serving Mass, and I know of one occasion when he heard the Confession of a woman in German. He would never have done this if he hadn't understood her, and if she hadn't understood his questions and answers.

When Pope John XXIII died, Padre Pio even knew who was going to be the next Pope. Padre Eusebio says that they used to tease him: "Who is going to be the next Pope?" Finally one day he just gave up and said: "Oh, Montini." Montini became Pope Paul VI.

Padre Pio didn't have all the answers. Once a woman came here with her husband from Long Island. She was dying of cancer, and she knew it. She was the mother of several children. She said: "There is a new medicine. Should I try it?" I went to Padre Pio and told him that she was the mother of children and that she was very with sick with cancer and wanted to try this cure. He said very humbly and touchingly: "My son, I don't know."

He did know—and he said this—when he would die. When the new church of Our Lady of Grace was finished in 1959, Mrs. Josephine Bove, of Naples, was upset. She thought that because the new church was finished, that might be his sign-off. He said to her: "I will die when they build the crypt." The crypt [beneath the church, where he is now buried] was not finished when the church was built. It was left abandoned for many years. Only in 1968 did they begin the finishing touches on the floor and walls. The work was begun again and completed and was blessed on Sunday, September 22. How many hours later did Padre Pio die? Fifteen hours later, at 2:30 in the morning of September 23. He also told Pietruccio—you know the blind Pietruccio—that he, Padre Pio, would die during his eighty-first year of life, which he did. When he died, he was eighty-one and four months.

[*Claims of miracles through Padre Pio's intercession were not made daily; yet over the span of eighty years, and after his death, their number seems to be legion. I asked Father Joseph Pius if he ever witnessed a miracle.*]

I have never witnessed a miracle. I was with Padre Pio when people would come and thank him for things that might be classified as miracles. But actually to be with him, side by side, for example, and see him give sight to the blind—I have never seen that. But I have seen many documented cases of cures worked by his hands, through his intercession. Cancers that disappear are pretty spectacular.

Probably the most spectacular are the miracles of the soul, when people suddenly converted their lives. I know a man who after sixty-five years without God began going to Mass every day—every day, not only every Sunday—and receiving Holy Communion. I suppose that these are the great miracles.

[*I asked him if he ever witnessed a case of Padre Pio's bilocation.*]

One case involved Raffaelina Russo, who is mentioned in the first volume of Padre Pio's *Letters*. She was a very good Tertiary [member of the Secular Franciscans, or Third Order of St. Francis]. She is the one who brought him up to the friary in a donkey cart when he first came here. She was very close to him.

Raffaelina's niece told me that one evening Raffaelina went into the guest quarters. Two or three other people were present. Padre Pio had his arms folded and his head down. He remained like that, motionless, for a long time. Suddenly he sat up and rejoined the group. They said: "Where have you been?"

He said: "I was at home, giving my greetings to my father. I was in Rome with my sister [in the convent]. And I was in [Jamaica] New York with my brother."

About two years before Padre Pio died, I met a very humble woman from New York who came to the friary. She was perfectly normal, not a fanatic. She said that she had been critically ill, with a tumor on her throat. She was not expected to live. She told me that she had invoked Padre Pio's aid. Suddenly he was at the foot of her bed and blessed her. He said: "Get up." She got up and came to San Giovanni Rotondo, completely cured. I wouldn't have believed it if I hadn't seen it.

[*Documentation exists proving the devil's physical assaults against Padre Pio. I asked Father Bill if he ever experience any such encounters.*]

In July of 1964 there was a possessed woman being exorcised at San Giovanni Rotondo. Padre Pio came through the church that morning to give his general blessing to the women, as he usually did after hearing Confessions. This woman started to speak, but in an unnatural bass voice, saying: "Padre Pio, I'll see you tonight."

People wrote it off, as if she was a little cracked in the head, talking to Padre Pio in that manner. That night . . . Think of the noise—the level of the noise—which there must have been! The superior was awakened by a tremendous noise from Padre Pio's room. He rushed in. Padre Pio was on the floor in his night clothes, but with a pillow under his head, bleeding from his forehead. His face was cut above the right eyebrow. His eyes were black, and under the eyes was all black. He looked like he took charcoal and underlined his eyes. His shoulders were terribly bruised. He was like that for a week.

The superior said: "Padre, how did you get there? Who put the pillow under your head?"

He answered: "La Madonna."

That morning the Capuchins gave out the story that Padre Pio had got up during the night and had fallen. He wasn't able to come down for Mass for a week. The friars were criticized by some fanatical women for not having assisted Padre Pio.

We believed him. The exorcism continued the next day. The devil was challenged by the priest, and the devil answered: "Last night I was up to see that old man upstairs. I hate him so much because he is a fountain of faith. I would have done much more, except the White Lady stopped me and forbade me." I think they were the exact words the devil used. Therefore, we have the two things which are now connected: Padre Pio said that Our Lady put the pillow under his head, and the devil said that he would have done much more except the Madonna had stopped him.

About two years later a woman went to Confession to Padre Pio. She said to him: "Padre, the last time I was here was when that little devil hurt you so much."

"Little devil!" he said. "He wasn't little at all. He had the hooves of Lucifer to beat me with." During the exorcism the devil had said something about himself having the hooves of Lucifer to attack Padre Pio with.

Occasionally Padre Pio would be bounced out of his chair onto the floor. One morning Padre Onorato and I had gone down to have coffee. This was perfectly normal, because we would leave Padre Pio in his easy chair with a buzzer strapped around the arm of the chair, so that he would just have to make a hand motion in order to call for help. Everything was normal. In that space of five minutes Padre Onorato came back upstairs and heard Padre Pio yelling: "Help me! Help me!"

He rushed into the room. There was Padre Pio on the floor. The devil had come in and started the battle, and had knocked him onto the floor.

The last month of his life he was constantly confronted with the presence of the devil. He would sit on the veranda next to his room, praying the rosary. It's a wonder the rosary didn't take roots in his fingers, because he was never without it. He would look around in a semi-circle, watching something that would rotate around him. It would make you eerie, because you knew he was seeing something. That wasn't something that happened just once, as if he happened to be looking at a piece of dust rolling on the floor. This was almost every day. Once Padre Mariano asked him what he saw. He just said: "I see a head." But I know it was the devil.

In one instance his confessor, Padre Raffaele, got up. Padre Pio hollered at him: "Turn around!" The devil had gone at him, and Padre Pio wanted to see if the devil was clutching at the back of Padre Raffaele's habit. We didn't see anything.

Once he was staring at my feet in such a way that I was sure the devil was crawling on me, or the image of the devil. It made me terribly eerie. I never saw anything or felt anything, but I could see Padre Pio visually seeing this thing that was with him constantly for the last months of his life. I think the devil was his constant companion, physically beating him.

When the devil couldn't get at Padre Pio, he attacked his

works. The devil once said that very thing: "I can no longer hurt Padre Pio personally, but I will hurt his works."

As far back as Pietrelcina [Padre Pio's home town], not only in the seminary when he was not yet ordained but even in Michaele's house [Michaele was his brother] where Padre Pio slept, you could see the marks of the devil on the wall—the claw marks and the ink marks. This went on for his whole life, right until the day of his death, even in physical combat.

Padre Pio was very alert to unexpected movements or sounds. He once said (I think it was in one of his letters) that the devil appeared to him in all shapes.

Some say (but I never saw this personally) that he had a fear, for instance, of even a mouse, because the devil would start as a mouse and then turn into a claw or something. It would go for his eyes. It's fantastic. To encounter Padre Pio was like reading medieval history—not only the devil getting at him, but I saw two possessed persons at San Giovanni Rotondo.

The first was during a summer's evening. There was a commotion in the piazza. As I left the church, I was on my way to buy an ice cream on a hot summer night, not thinking anything about a devil. I returned to the friary, and there was a priest sprinkling holy water on a young woman in her thirties. She exhibited a strength that you would have to say was superhuman. Two men could not hold her in the chair. Her hair and scarf were all dissheveled, her clothes were pulled apart, her shoes were off. She would rise up out of the chair and throw the men back. They would grab her again and push her down, but she would throw them back again. Her strength! It was a horsepower that she had—an animal power.

The minute Padre Pio came in front of her, it was as if she were dead. There was no movement, there was no sound, there was nothing. He blessed her and went on. Then it started in a way that actually scared me to see her, because you saw something that wasn't human. It was frightening, because I had not seen anything like that in my life. The minute he left her, she went back to the old style of hooting and howling and showing her superhuman force.

The second case was that of a woman whom the devil used to go into animal movements. I saw that. The woman was placed on a pew in the church, waiting for Padre Pio's blessing. When he came through and blessed her, there was not a single sound. But she was twisting like a snake in agony. It was the most fantastic thing to see. She could not have been an actress, because she could not have kept up the motion uninterruptedly for so long. Padre Carmelo told everyone to leave. Padre Carmelo was watching her, because he understood very well what was wrong with the woman—that it was not something physical.

A third case I didn't see myself, but it is terribly interesting. There was a boy in Milan who was a perfectly normal child. Suddenly at the age of six he stopped speaking. They couldn't get a word out of him. His mother, if I'm not mistaken, was a widow. She took him to every specialist in Milan and spent all she had on him. No one could do anything for him. There was no explanation why he couldn't speak. Physically he was perfect.

Six years passed, and they brought him to Padre Pio. They started to relate that he had been to all kinds of doctors and specialists. Padre Pio interrupted: "This is not a thing for medicine."

He made the Sign of the Cross over the boy, and the boy immediately began to speak. It was the devil that had held his tongue. This is a fact that can be attested to by the friars who were with Padre Pio, and by the people who were in the hallway at the time.

I can't explain these things. Even if I would be a theologian, I think that a person would have to be a specialist in ascetical theology. It's out of vogue today to believe in the devil, but the devil exists. He has a greater part in our lives than we give him credit for.

Cases of diabolical possession at San Giovanni Rotondo weren't very common. I don't want to give you the idea that this was happening every day. I was there for four or five years, and I saw only two cases that I could spot which were actual possession and not obsession [an external, physical attack].

[*On the other end of the angelic spectrum we have the Guardian Angels. Padre Pio spoke frequently about them. I asked Father Joseph Pius if it were true that Padre Pio actually had their good services.*]

It's a fact. It's definitely a fact. Even in the supernatural order the soul has to be informed. Was Padre Pio informed by the Guardian Angel? I don't know how it worked, but I can tell you that it did work. I do know that Padre Pio was in great cahoots with the angels.

There was a woman once who went to Padre Pio. She said: "Did my Guardian Angel really come to you?" and he told her: "Your Guardian Angel is much more obedient than you are."

Father Dominic Meyer [an American Capuchin priest and doctor of theology, who for twelve years was secretary to Padre Pio], at first didn't "dig" this business about Padre Pio's Guardian Angel. But he heard the stories. One morning he saw Padre Pio particularly tired. He asked: "Didn't you sleep well? Did you get any rest last night?"

Padre Pio answered him: "The Guardian Angels kept me up all night—one message after another."

Father Dominic! Good Lord! I heard that from *him*! Now I have to believe it. He said that it will take people of great faith to appreciate Padre Pio, because of all that went on with him. Father Dominic said that Padre Pio was too extraordinary for our time.

One day a woman who lives in San Giovanni Rotondo went on a trip to Rome. She had been in the habit of coming after the evening Benediction to his window with the group of people to wave goodnight. It was a touching scene. That evening he opened the window as usual, and he gave his blessing as usual. Then he stopped. I was standing arm in arm with Padre Pio. I could see him looking and listening to someone right in front of him, whom I couldn't see. He turned to me and said: "Where is Martha Gemsch tonight?"

When she returned from her trip I questioned her: "You sent your Guardian Angel to Padre Pio when you were away, didn't you?"

She answered: "Yes." She had sent her Guardian Angel after

the evening blessing, which she had not been able to attend. Actually Padre Pio saw the reality of it. I know only the facts— that she was away from the town, and then I had her confirmation of what ensued.

[*I inquired about Padre Pio's other devotions, especially to the Poor Souls in Purgatory.*]

You know how many people visited Padre Pio each day— every year? Well, Padre Pio once said that there were more souls of the dead who come up that road than souls of the living. The stories about these departed souls are fantastic.

One day a car with three or four Capuchins overturned in northern Italy and all were killed. The Capuchins at San Giovanni Rotondo told Padre Pio what had happened, and they asked for his prayers. But it seems quite clear from his reaction that he had already known that they were dead. Evidently he had seen them that night.

When the Church took away some indulgences, he was surprised. He said: "Now who will think of the Holy Souls? Pray hard for them every day." He was in frequent conversation with them. I am quite sure that certain people who died were permitted to go to Padre Pio and request certain things for their families.

His principal devotion was to the Eucharist. Then there was his devotion to Our Blessed Mother, and to St. Joseph, whom he prayed to every day, in particular in the last months of his life. We gave Padre Pio a picture of St. Joseph which he said he wanted. We had to put it by the window on the veranda as he requested. He stopped there in front of that picture every day at four o'clock for the last two or three months before he died. At the time we didn't understand that he was praying for a good death.

He also had devotion to many of the saints. His favorite was St. Francis of Assisi, whom he saw very often in apparition. He had devotion to St. Dominic and St. Catherine of Siena, because of the rosary. He began many of his letter with "J.M.J.D.F.C." These letters mean: "Jesus, Mary, Joseph, Dominic, Francis and Catherine."

Padre Pio prayed every day for the Pope. Padre Pellegrino, who was his night assistant, said that Padre Pio would get up at two o'clock in the morning and then sit in his easy chair (which wasn't very easy, I'll tell you!). The lamp had to be draped, because the light would bother his eyes. But the drape had to be open so that a ray of light could hit the Pope's picture which was always on his desk. Until the ray of light hit the Pope's picture, and until part of that light came onto the clock, he was never satisfied. That is how he would begin his day: praying for the Holy Father.

Also he had the utmost respect—devotion, if you will—for the religious habit. He was of the old school, when the friars wore their night habits instead of pajamas. When Father Guardian [the superior] dispensed him from wearing the night habit, he cried. He wanted to die in it. When he was dying, he got up and dressed in it. He then sat down on the veranda, wearing it, knowing very well that the end was coming, and he did die in it.

He wouldn't receive priests who came to him without the habit. I don't know if I'd criticize them, but a lot of people went as a joke to see if he knew supernaturally what was going on—priests without their habits. He would say: "Put on your habit. Then come back and I will hear your Confession." They were then delighted that he knew.

[I asked Father Joseph Pius how Padre Pio could serve as an inspiration to people who have never met him.]

He can be the door that opens to a new life of faith—a door that reveals religion to people, that leads to peace within people's souls, even to eternal salvation.

The last chapter on Padre Pio can never be written, but it will take great faith on our part to believe what Padre Pio has accomplished. His town is growing. It is really a city. He will never just be a statue put on the shelf to collect dust. He said one striking thing: "One day men will doubt that I existed." I suppose in the time of anti-Christ they will try to erase his figure, because he is so vitally alive, and he is a man of our own time, historically and scientifically. He has been documented and photographed. Just meeting him could mean eternal salvation for people.

Some people think they can't get close to God, but they can get close to God through him. That will never stop. The fact that he is dead makes no difference at all. When you see the thousands of people (last year some estimated three million!), they can't all be fanatics and tourists. We will never be finished with Padre Pio till the end of time.

Now add the dimension of Padre Pio's mysticism. I think he was the greatest mystic in the history of the Church. His *Letters*, although only recently published in Italian and English, show him to be a great mystic—something we never realized. We knew that he was a great saint, but we never suspected that the degree of his mysticism was so elevated.

As soon as the *Letters* were published, Padre Bernardino, the postulator general for the Capuchins, brought a copy to Father Vittorio, the Carmelite Father who is one of the most famous authorities in the world on mysticism. Father Vittorio read the book, and he was just amazed.

To meet Padre Pio, even after his death, is to find heaven, because that is where Padre Pio will lead us. I have never met anyone who has been lukewarm in reaction to the name of Padre Pio. Either they hate him or they love him. They hate him in the sense that "this is all hocus-pocus—Let's get out of here!" or they are completely flabbergasted by him.

13. Alfonso D'Artega
Rome

Tens of thousands of GI's visited Padre Pio during World War II, including Alfonso D'Artega. He has achieved international renown as a composer and symphony conductor. Besides the personal blessings he received from Padre Pio, D'Artega's testimony adds to the strange but apparently true accounts of "the flying monk"—Padre Pio's appearance or appearances during the war to the crew of fighters and bombers in full flight. Luigi Barzini wrote a book, The Italians, *and in it he describes this incident (or similar incidents) of Padre Pio being seen by flyers during World War II. Magazine articles also add to the credibility of this fact, as do the family letters of Father Dominic Meyer, Padre Pio's secretary for twelve years—a man not readily given to believe and write about mere gossip.—JS*

*   *   *

During the War in 1944 and 1945 I was in Special Services in the Air Force. I was stationed at the airfield in Amendola, near San Giovanni Rotondo. I had heard about Padre Pio before the war, but while I was at Amendola, our little mascot, a ten-year-old boy Alberto Calalla, told me quite a few miraculous things about this very holy friar up there in San Giovanni Rotondo. I knew that Padre Pio was not far away.

One evening some flyers who had taken part in a mission were talking among themselves. One of the pilots said: "I saw that phantom fly again." We were having drinks, and at first I didn't know what they were talking about. Then another man made pertinent remarks about the phantom flying, but I didn't know that they meant Padre Pio. I thought that maybe they had too many drinks, until about a week later. One chap (not a pilot but a member of the crew) was perfectly sober. He said that there was a photographer taking pictures of the planes as they landed from their missions. One of the planes was pretty badly hurt, and the men were dazed. They had landed their planes still with their bombs—they had not been jettisoned. They should have dropped the bombs somewhere on the way in the Adriatic.

This chap explained that he had been flying, when all of a sudden in front of him there was a figure of a monk, flying as fast as the plane, waving his arms. [Technically, Capuchins are friars, not monks.] The copilot also saw it. So they didn't drop the bombs on the way back, because they were afraid. They sort of froze when they saw this figure. Naturally, in briefing, when they made their report they were bawled out for not having dropped the bombs, endangering the rest of the crew.

At the time there was also a fellow by the name of Pope, who was a pilot. I remember the name distinctly. Pope told Andrews, a friend of mine who was in the ground crew, that *he* had seen this phantom flyer. Pope was a fighter pilot, so his plane didn't have any bombs, but he saw the figure of the "flying monk." He didn't describe him as a Capuchin; he said he had a brown robe. Unfortunately Pope was killed.

The curiosity of the other pilots from these briefings prompted one particular chap to make a trip to San Giovanni Rotondo in a jeep. He verified the fact that he had seen Padre Pio in the sky. I don't know what that chap's name is.

I also heard another flyer, a young man from Chicago, say that he saw Padre Pio up there in the sky. He did not verify the fact that it was Padre Pio until he saw a picture of him. He was Protestant at the time. He became a Catholic and then a priest.

Time passed. Finally in 1964 restrictions on Padre Pio had been lifted and he was available again to be seen. Not realizing that a routine had to be followed for a person to confess to Padre Pio [by that time tickets had to be obtained] my wife and I went to San Giovanni Rotondo. We allowed only two days. I went to the window where Padre Vincenzo gave out the tickets. He said: "You have to wait five days."

I thought that by this time I knew enough Italian to be able to confess to Padre Pio, and I had a recording session scheduled here in Rome. When Padre Vincenzo said that I'd have to wait for five days, I was so disappointed that I almost cried. I told him that this was the first opportunity I had. I finally got a ticket to go to Confession, but I couldn't use it. When I left that little gangway, I was despondent. I walked out.

A man came across the street and came up to me and said: "You probably came here to see Padre Pio."

I said: "Of course."

He said: "Well, have you been to Confession?"

I said: "No. I'm very disappointed. I just got a ticket, but I can't use it."

He said: "Well, I have a ticket. You can go to Confession with this."

I was very surprised. I said: "Why don't you use it? What's connected with it?"

He said: "I'll give it to you. I tried to give it to ten others, but nobody wants it. Take it." I took it immediately.

I went back to Padre Vincenzo, who was just closing the window. I said: "Father, look. I was here before, and I told you I'm a foreigner, and I have come here to San Giovanni Rotondo. I have never been to Confession here. I want to confess now."

He said: "You cannot take another person's ticket." Just like that. You *could* use other people's tickets—I found that out later. But he looked around and said: "I don't see anybody. Maybe Padre Pio wants to see you."

I said: "When does this happen?"

He said: "In an hour." I almost fell over.

Within an hour I was right in front of Padre Pio, shaking, trembling. But he was so sweet, so nice. He gave me absolution right away, even with all my mistakes. That brought me very close to him. This is not a coincidence.

I will tell you of another episode which brought me closer again. I had a great desire to serve Padre Pio's Mass. One day I went to the friary and they said: "You know, there are *prenotati* [reservations], and so on, and all the men who serve Mass are from around here, and they have to know you, and we have to know you. . . ."

I said: "I'm from Rome. Isn't it possible?" I even had written letters from Rome, but nothing happened.

Then in May 1965 the American Women's Club of Santa Suzanna was going to San Giovanni Rotondo on a tour. At the last minute I made up my mind to go along with all the women.

The door opened, and I ran in—woosh—with all the women, and landed in the front row. I had a briefcase with something I wanted Padre Pio to bless: a Mass that I wrote for President J. F. Kennedy, and I wanted Padre Pio to bless it. Oh, how I wished that I could be at the altar. I was looking at the altar. Just two minutes were lacking before Mass.

All of a sudden a man came out of the sacristy. He made a whole turn and came right in front of me. He stood right over me and said: "Where is Alfonso lo Mexicano?" Everybody knows me as being Spanish or American, but nobody knows that I was born in Mexico. I looked up at him and said: "I'm Alfonso." He said: "Come on."

I was so excited that I climbed over the Communion rail and followed him. Just then Padre Pio was coming out. I looked at him and he looked at me as if to say: "I've been expecting you." The man rang the bell, and I walked with Padre Pio and served his Mass. Now explain that!

Whoever served Mass had the privilege of kneeling alongside of him. So there I was. Padre Pio had his head down, with his cappuccio [cowl, or hood] up over it. All I could hear was the tick-tock-tock of the clock. I had my book with me, the life of Kennedy in music. Padre Pio reached over, put his hand on it, and blessed it, as if I . . . Then it was over.

Finally I went outside and met the man who had called me. I asked him: "How did this happen?" His name was Giovanni Siena, a writer. He said: "In Padre Pio's life we never know anything. We just *do,* and all of a sudden things happen."

That was Wednesday morning. The man who usually served Mass on Wednesdays was Gerardo DeCaro, an attorney in Foggia. He and Padre Pio are close friends. Gerardo has served Mass every Wednesday for many years—ten. He still serves on Wednesday morning. He overslept!

All this led me to do more for Padre Pio, by composing and directing [for the Rome Symphony Orchestra] the music for the famous movie "Fifty Years of Thorns and Roses." I became involved in it by meeting three truck drivers in California. I met Mrs. Wenzel, who financed the film, in Zurich. My passport had expired, and this lady had heard about me. It seems to be all a plan how one gets pulled into this circle by Padre Pio. Imagine! Of all the musicians of the world I was the only one chosen to play the organ in the film beneath Padre Pio's voice. I had never directed a picture in my life. Padre Pio helped me to put it together somehow. Things don't just happen like that.

Is it all coincidence? No! There were no coincidences in Padre Pio's life. I think everything had a pattern. Father Joseph Pius too will tell you that. Padre Pio selected you, he selected us, before we even arrived. He selected me long ago to do what I have done in my own humble way, long before I knew anything about it.

14. Agnese Stump
Voghera

Voghera is a city in northern Italy. Miss Stump is Italian, but of Swiss-German extraction. Because the documentation in her case is so clear and complete, the miracle she has described may be used in Padre Pio's canonization process. I began by asking how she first heard about Padre Pio. —JS

* * *

I first heard of Padre Pio when I was a little girl, six or seven. I had a friend at school whose grandmother used to visit him. Every time I visited her home, I would notice a picture of Padre Pio. From that time onward I learned more and more about him. I felt very close to him.

Also, my aunt is very devoted to Padre Pio. Through her example I always prayed to Padre Pio, and he helped me not only in school but also in my every day life, even though I never had the joy of meeting him during his lifetime.

When I was about twenty, I began to feel occasional pains in my left knee. I went to our family doctor, and he told me it was arthritis. He gave me an injection and pills. The pain came and went, so I agreed it was arthritis. I didn't pay any more attention to it. I would feel the pain only if I would touch my knee or bump it against something.

One day I twisted my ankle. The pain was very sharp and caused me to limp. Again I went to the doctor, and he took an X ray which revealed a tumor. However, he said he couldn't help me because he wasn't a specialist. He advised me to go to Tortona, to Doctor Rinaldi, a specialist in orthopedics.

Doctor Rinaldi diagnosed it as "neoplasm of the tibia in the left knee." He said I should be operated on right away to prevent it from spreading, but I didn't want to believe him. I didn't like the idea of an operation. Until then I had not even had a headache, so it didn't seem possible that a serious illness could have stricken me. So I went to Milan to see Doctor Poli. He said the same thing as Doctor Rinaldi. He confirmed that I had to be operated on, but I didn't want to believe him either.

On December 22, 1967, I told my father and brother to go down to Padre Pio and ask him if I should be operated on. They arrived at San Giovanni Rotondo on Christmas Eve and went to Confession to him. He said to them: "Yes, go ahead and have the operation. Don't be afraid. Nothing will be done without my hand. I will assist Agnese in my prayers and guide the hand that operates on her."

On January 2, 1968, I entered the hospital in Tortona and was operated on. I remained in the hospital with a cast on for the whole month. Then I returned home. My leg was in a cast, and I used crutches, but the operation was a success. For two months I went back to Tortona for checkups. The doctor took more X rays and found that everything was fine. I did not have to take any medication other than vitamins.

Everything was coming along well. They took the cast off my leg and put on a bandage and gave me exercises. This was until October. Then the pains came back again, and again I visited the doctor and he said that the condition had recurred. He advised another operation. What a blow! All my hopes of the previous months were shattered.

I was operated on again in Tortona by Doctor Rinaldi. He removed the whole tumor and put the cast back on. Then they removed a piece of bone and sent it to Pavia, Milan, and Genoa for histological examination. The diagnosis we received was that sarcogenous [malignant] cancer had developed into myelopathy [cancer of the bone marrow].

The bone was all eaten up and looked like a black sponge. I couldn't stand on my left leg, because there was nothing left of the bone to support me. The bone was full of pus. But the doctor operated on me and cleaned out the pus. That left a small cavity.

From January to October the bone grew again and the cavity

filled up, but then the tumor emerged again in the same spot. This second tumor was worse than the first—the cancer had entered my blood stream. The doctor wanted to amputate my leg before it got any worse and spread any further throughout my body. I said: "No, I don't want that." I told Doctor Rinaldi: "I have to make a novena to Padre Pio." So I went home. Doctor Rinaldi was angry with me and didn't even say goodbye. I began my novena and promised to accept the doctor's decision as God's will. Even if they had to amputate my leg, I would accept it because it was for my benefit.

I went for yet another checkup—this time to Doctor Carnacchia. He said that he did not recommend amputation, but that he would prescribe treatment which would make my leg rigid. I refused that and went home. I was so sure that Padre Pio would cure me.

On November 30 I went to Milan to see another doctor, Doctor Frontino. He was an assistant to Doctor Scaglietti of Florence. This doctor didn't know what to do. He said that he would make his decision when I was on the operating table at the hospital, where he had special instruments. Only then would he be able to decide what to do—to amputate the leg or save it. However, he knew that some kind of an operation was necessary. Until then I had been walking with a cane; it was his opinion that without an operation I would not be able to walk at all. My leg couldn't support me. I went back home and did nothing.

On December 20 I visited the tomb of Padre Pio. Of course I could not see him, but neither could I be convinced that he could be lying under that cold gray marble stone. I felt his living presence within me and in every corner of that little crypt.

I went to the Home for the Relief of Suffering to see Doctor Ficola. My leg was in a partial cast. He advised surgery which would give me partial use of my knee. I didn't accept that. Absolutely no more operations!

In the meantime, I prayed constantly to Padre Pio. One night I dreamed of him. It seemed that I went to him using my cane, my leg in a cast. He received me in a room where he received pilgrims. In the dream I told him that my leg was in a cast and in pain. He looked at me, smiled, and winked at me. I kissed his hands, but they didn't have any stigmata. I could see no open wound or blood.

I kissed his cheek, and he was laughing. There were so many people in this room. He took me by the arm and we walked arm-in-arm toward the door. I noticed that I had left my crutches in the corner. I said: "Look, Padre! I have left my crutches in the corner and I'm walking toward the door without them." I said: "I am going back to get my crutches."

He said: "What do you want them for? You don't need them." With that, I woke up.

After supper, I saw that I was walking around using only my cane. Until that time I couldn't do anything without crutches, because I am heavy. I told my brother George that I was walking around with only a cane and that I couldn't feel much weight.

On April 25, 1969, I threw away the cane. I felt as though someone had ordered me to throw it away. The doctor removed the cast, and I did not need any therapy, although I did exercise a bit to stimulate the movement in my legs. For a year and a half I had worn the cast. Then I began to walk a little with the cane for support, and then a little every day without the cane. Now I don't use it at all.

When I first began to walk again, the first thing I did was to go to San Giovanni Rotondo. Doctor Ficola took X rays and said that the bone was normal. He signed an affidavit that the damaged bone was now normal healthy bone. He left me a written statement that this could be explained only by a miracle: healthy good bone had grown from a bone which had been consumed.

I went back to the doctor who had operated on me. He took more X rays. He was surprised, and he said the same thing: "It is a miracle." He began to cry when he saw the X rays and realized that it was a miracle. He said: "This is the first miracle which I have witnessed since Padre Pio's death." He called in all the doctors and said to them: "Come and look at the miracle woman who has received the first miracle since Padre Pio's death."

The doctor who operated on me is not Catholic. He never went to church—he was far away from the church. He admitted that Padre Pio had been a fighter for me. He said: "But I am happy to have an opponent like Padre Pio."

I go to San Giovanni Rotondo every year. I promised Padre Pio: "Padre, if I will be able to walk again, every year I will go down to San Giovanni Rotondo." Even if I hadn't promised that, I would go there anyway. But now I can make the stairs of the crypt without help and I can thank Padre Pio on my knees at his tomb.

15. Cleonice Morcaldi
San Giovanni Rotondo

Miss Morcaldi is one of the "old guard," a resident of San Giovanni Rotondo for fifty years and very dear spiritual daughter of Padre Pio. She is the niece of Francesco Morcaldi, former mayor of the town.—JS

* * *

Padre Pio received the stigmata while he was in Pietrelcina [his hometown, where he lived with his family in 1910 because of poor health. These wounds appeared and disappeared until 1918, when they remained visible until his death in 1968]. After he came to San Giovanni Rotondo, initially he didn't wear gloves to cover the wounds. Instead he would wrap his hands in the tip of his mantle in order to hide his hands. Gradually everyone came to know that he had been stigmatized.

He prayed and prayed: "Jesus take away these wounds." Jesus did not answer his prayer, because the world had to see with their own eyes that God had sent us another crucifixion—otherwise the world would not believe. God sent us in this century this great soul; Padre Pio became a co-redeemer with Christ. [See Colossians 1:24: "Even now I find joy in the suffering I endure for you. In my own flesh I fill up what is lacking in the sufferings of Christ for the sake of his body, the Church." Frequently I heard priests and laity cite this Scripture quote to describe Padre Pio's ministry and mission.]

Every year the wounds would continue to spread more and more, and his hands would be covered with crusts which would reach to the base of his fingers. I kissed Padre Pio's fingers for ten years while he was not wearing gloves. [My understanding is that the wounds themselves did not become larger. However, they seemed to become larger because they constantly oozed blood which spread across his hands and formed hard crusts. Pictures of him at Mass might lead a person to think that the wounds covered the entire palms of his hands. The actual holes were about as big as a penny.]

Before the new church was built in 1959, Padre Pio celebrated Mass in the small church. I was seated very near him. After Mass he would pass his hand along the Communion rail, and he would let me kiss his fingers. The crusts on his hands were very hard, pointed, and needle-sharp. Everyone could see the wounds on the palms and backs of his hands when the Father would turn during Mass.

One day a woman in the crowd, upon seeing him, started to scream: "Padre Pio, Padre Pio, please heal me, heal me. I am sick. I have gone to many hospitals, but no one seems to help me." The people were saying to the woman: "Keep quiet." But Padre Pio went near her, just as Jesus went to the blind man in the Gospel when the people told him to keep quiet. Padre Pio asked her: "What do you want?"

She replied: "I am sick. I am a poor mother. I have children." And Padre Pio said: "My daughter, I too . . . I was born sick. I have lived sick." Then he turned to the friar who was with him and said: "I'll die healthy." [He used the word *sano*, which can be translated "healthy" or "whole." It was probably a cryptic reference to the disappearance of the stigmata at the time of his death. He had no wounds when he died; he died suffering no illness. The cause of his death was a heart attack from asthma.] We saw him. He had nothing. During his last Mass, the day before he died, we saw Padre Pio's hands cured of his wounds. The sleeves of the alb were pulled back. The palms and backs of his hands were very smooth, like the hand of a healthy new-born child. His hands were very white and shiny like marble, beautifully clean, whole and intact. In a moment, just as God had wounded him, God healed him. It impressed us very much.

I had asked Padre Pio: "What is your Mass?" It could last for three hours. Before I came here in 1934, the Mass lasted two and a half hours or more. He answered me: "It is an exchange between me and Jesus."

I asked him: "Father, don't you get tired, always standing on those feet of yours covered with wounds?" He replied: "I am not standing on my feet."

I said: "But Father, I see you standing on your feet." I thought: Where could he be standing if not on his feet? What can this be? I could see him. To us children he talked a little more freely, perhaps revealing a little more. With his confreres he did not speak very much about these things—he was more shy.

I turned to him and said: "Then, Padre, if you are not standing on your feet, you must be on the cross of Jesus. You must be suspended from the cross." And he said: "Is it only now that you see this? Don't you know that I am on the cross?"

One day a student from the university came to see his fiancée. She said to him: "You must come to see the Mass of Padre Pio. You must meet Padre Pio. Otherwise I will not marry you."

This student went to Padre Pio's Mass. He stood in the back of the church, watching. He went to Mass on the second, third, and fourth day. After a week he began crying and crying. Finally he went to see Padre Pio in the sacristy. Padre Pio said to him: "Thank God for what you have seen. And don't say anything to anyone. God's secrets are kept in the heart."

The young man, without having said anything to Padre Pio, understood that Padre Pio had seen everything in him. He said to Padre Pio: "Yes, Father, I saw you on the altar all crowned with thorns. First I saw three crowns of thorns, and then something like a bonnet of thorns."

Padre Pio said again: "Don't say anything to anyone. Go home and thank God, and don't say anything to anyone." But his fiancée told us everything. She said that he had seen Padre Pio every morning crowned with thorns and his face all dripping blood, but with such a serene, beautiful expression on his face. So sweet was this expression that the man couldn't help being moved and could not help crying.

I believed everything he said, but I wanted to go to Padre Pio to ask him personally if it were true. I went to his confessional. "Please, Father," I said, "tell me if it is true—what that young man is saying. That young man said that he sees the thorns on your head. Is that true?"

Padre Pio said: "Do you have any doubt? You are like St. Thomas. You don't believe."

I didn't want to be like St. Thomas, so I questioned him no further. I knew he did not like to speak very much. I prayed to the Mother of God: "Madonna, please let Padre Pio tell me if this is true, that there is this crown of thorns."

I let a long time pass by. One day in Confession I said: "Father, that crown of thorns—do you wear it in all your Masses? During the time of Mass do you keep that on your head?"

He said: "How many things you want to know! Yes, I wear it before and even after the Mass, because I can never take off that diadem which is the crown of thorns that God has put on me— before Mass, during Mass, day and night.

Sometimes Padre Pio would tremble when he went to the altar. Once during my Confession [his spiritual children commonly used this occasion to ask him personal questions not connected with Confession], I asked him: "Do you tremble because you have to suffer?"

"No," he said, "it is not because of what I have to suffer, but because of what I have to offer. Don't you realize the mystery of the Mass? We are the butchers who slaughter the victim, Jesus, to offer Him to our heavenly Father in payment for our sins." That is why he trembled and wept all during his Masses.

I asked him why he cried. (It was not out of curiosity that I asked him these questions.) He said to me: "I don't wish to shed these small tears, but torrents of tears. Don't you see the great mystery of the Mass?"

One night in August it was very hot. I had sent him a white linen tunic. He always wore a tunic, no matter how hot it was or how much he was sweating. But when I sent him this tunic, he didn't return it to me. He kept it and used it for three days. Afterwards he sent it back to me. When I saw it, it was completely covered with blood. I said to myself: Madonna! It is just one flagellation! I said: "Father, you are all one big wound from head to foot."

And he said to me: "Isn't this for our glory? If there would not be any more room on my body to put another wound, we will make wound upon wound." On that tunic which he sent me, I saw that there were scabs of clotted blood, and inside the scabs were marks of wounds on top of each other.

I said: "You are the carnage of your own body!"

And he said: "Not of my own body, because I am made of flesh and blood like you. I offer my suffering to God because of the fruits it gives me. My pain gives glory to God, souls are saved, and it liberates souls from the fire of Purgatory."

Once he gave me a rosary and said: "Pray, pray, pray. We are going to empty Purgatory. We'll liberate all the souls in Purgatory." What can I say? He was prayer in person. He prayed night and day while he worked always with a rosary in his hand.

Just before he died, on September 20, I said: "Father, give me at least one word."

He said: "Love the Madonna. Make others love her, and recite her rosary. That is an armor against the evils of the world today."

I asked him: "Is the Madonna close to you?"

"A mother . . . " he said. "Can she be interested or disinterested in her children? All of paradise is near her."

The doctors advised the Father to take a little rest, at least on Sunday. He said: "We will all rest in paradise. Here we have to work. Here we cry. Here we suffer."

The last day before he died, in the morning of September 22, we kissed his hand, but he could hardly sit up straight in his chair. He had a cadaverous look. I said: "Padre, please say something to us."

He stretched out his arms and said: "I love everyone equally. Unfortunately I am not received kindly by everyone." He added: "Be constant and persevere in good, and we will arrive at the door of paradise."

I asked him: "Padre, does the demon Satan reign on earth?"

He said: "Only if they let him reign. A spirit cannot reign by itself if it is not united with the free will of man."

I said: "But the Madonna will help us in this century."

He said: "The Madonna is always ready to help. She is always ready to aid us. But we—do we realize that? Are we aware of that? Man never repents."

Once I said to him: "Padre, I have a strong desire to see the face of Jesus in my dreams."

He said: "Look at me! You deserve Jesus' reproach to Philip during the Last Supper. Philip said: 'Show me the Father', and Jesus said 'I have been with you such a long time and yet . . . ' " And Padre Pio added: "I have been with you such a long time and you do not see that Jesus is in me?"

At times, in humility, Padre Pio would say: "I am the worst delinquent on earth. The worst delinquent cannot compare himself with me. If you could see what I am really like inside, you would run away in fear."

He would say this in humility. But in the Holy Spirit he would say: "Do you want to see Jesus? Then look at me. Don't you yet know that he who sees me sees Jesus?" That is why, when I asked him how I should pray for him and what I should say to God for him, he replied: "That I be another Jesus, all Jesus, always Jesus." And that is what he has been—another Jesus.

So many people have come here for Confession, and Padre Pio would send them away. But he would torment them with remorse and would follow them with his prayers and sufferings. Ultimately they would return, fully repentent. He never lost a soul which God had sent him. He knew how to enter into the hearts of men. I know a doctor who visited Padre Pio. The doctor told me: "I came to San Giovanni Rotondo, but he told me: 'Go away, pig!' But I must return again, because he is torturing me. He is torturing my conscience at night."

Padre Pio said: "I torment their souls, and a fire devours them." The doctor returned and was welcomed by Padre Pio. The doctor became his staunchest promoter.

In the confessional many priests absolve with: "Very well, don't do it again." And the same sins are committed again and again. But the real children of Padre Pio returned truly reformed. That should be expected. Padre Pio was another Jesus; we cannot expect the same from all priests. Padre Pio could see the intimate soul. He said to me: "I know you inside and out, like you know yourself in the mirror."

We would go to Padre Pio always with fear and apprehension. There was no half measure with him, no minced words. But he had a love like Jesus, such tenderness for the poor and the suffering. Once he said: "God, give me the pain and suffering of my brothers."

The Holy Spirit has taken the words of Padre Pio and has made them enter into the hearts of men—into the hearts of men who have not known Jesus. Today at his tomb we see all people of all nations—Chinese, Indians, Japanese—who have never seen Padre Pio. Yet they are there, praying and weeping. Who spoke to them of Padre Pio? They have heard some things, but it is the Holy Spirit who has enlightened them. They come here because, I repeat, this is the century of Padre Pio.

16. Padre Raffaele, Capuchin Benevento

If for no other reason, this interview has importance from the length of time Padre Raffaele and Padre Pio lived together in San Giovanni Rotondo: thirty-five years. For thirteen of those years Padre Raffaele was the Father Guardian (local superior) of the friary.

Life in the friary and in the town was not always peaceful and serene. On occasion, although rarely, the zeal of the people who loved Padre Pio got out of hand, to the point of fanaticism, and of violence against people they suspected of being Padre Pio's "enemies." Because Padre Raffaele was superior, he was directly and immediately involved in the sequence of these events—he was not a casual observer.

Some people are shocked to learn that not everybody loved Padre Pio. At one time his own archbishop denounced him as a fraud. The Holy See itself might even appear as having been hostile to him by placing restrictions on his ministry among the people in 1923, 1933, and 1960. The voice of authority in the Church usually speaks through the chain of command. Therefore, the local superior of a community has a unique advantage when he recalls what has happened during his tenure of office.

During my interview with Padre Raffaele, and in my interview with Padre Clemente, which follows this one, I did not assume the role of an investigative journalist by digging into the facts of those turbulent times. I believe that Padre Pio's biographies provide a sufficient chronicle of those events. My intention was only to obtain the personal insights of Padre Raffaele and Padre Clemente relevant to their association with Padre Pio.

I will add here only one prefatory note of my own, not specifically verbalized by Padre Raffaele in this interview: Padre Pio's obedience and respect for Church authority at every level was immediate, absolute, uncompromising.

I began by asking Padre Raffaele some questions about Padre Pio's personal life, for example his daily routine.—JS

In his early priestly life, from 1930 to 1935, he would get up at three o'clock in the morning; but during the summer he would get up at five-thirty; in the winter, at six or six-thirty. He would celebrate Mass whenever his superiors would tell him.

After Mass he would hear Confessions until noon, or as late as twelve-thirty. Many times his superior had to call him out of the confessional and tell him to come to the refectory; otherwise he would be hearing Confessions all the time.

When he came for meals, he ate only a little. He would just take a nibble. Sometimes he would converse with us for about fifteen minutes or a half hour, and then he would go and take a little rest.

Vespers began at 2:30 p.m., and he would be with us for it. Then he would hear Confessions until the Angelus at six p.m. In the evening he would take a little something, maybe a cookie and a half glass of beer; but he never came to supper in the evening— never.

In his later years, generally he would not go to bed at all. When he would go to bed, he would keep his alarm set for about three o'clock, and he would sleep only about three hours at most. The rest of the night he remained in prayer.

[*I inquired about the friary itself: how old it was and when additions were made.*]

The old part of the friary was built centuries ago, in 1600. Then two additions were made in the last century. After the earthquake of 1939, I had the veranda built off Padre Pio's room. For two nights during its construction he and two friars slept in a little room under the little stairs. Then I had an ambulance brought from the hospital and parked it in the friary garden. It was in that ambulance that he slept for almost a month.

[*At this point I changed my line of questions to inquire about the tempests that had swirled around Padre Pio: Why were any restrictions at all imposed on Padre Pio?*]

To avoid the crowds. Once in a while orders and counter- orders would come in to try to control the situation; the people never took those orders lying down. At first he was forbidden to celebrate Mass in public; then he was suspended from all activity among the people. However, he continued to celebrate Mass privately, in the friary. The friars protested this restriction. For this reason, and also to keep the crowd from gossiping, Padre Pio was later allowed to offer Mass in public.

At this time the Father Provincial warned me to tell Padre Pio to shorten the time it took him for Mass. [In the 1920s, Padre Pio's Mass occasionally took two or three hours.] This directive always came from Rome: that Padre Pio should shorten the time of his Mass to a half hour. It was impossible for him to shorten the Mass, because he was absorbed in prayer. He used to say: "I don't know how long it takes me. I'm not aware of the time."

How could I stop him? Would I go up to him with a red flag and say: "Hey, shorten the Mass! It's too long!"?

Later on it was not possible for him to take several hours. His heart was weak. His Mass would take maybe thirty-five to forty-five minutes. In 1960 his Mass lasted about forty-five minutes to an hour—not less than thirty minutes. He couldn't stand on his feet any longer than that.

In 1923 and 1924 the people began to make threats, because an order had come for Padre Pio to be removed from the friary [that is, he would be transferred, possibly to another Italian Province, to Spain, or even to New York City!]. The crowd was armed. That is why the Holy See assumed responsibility for the situation and rescinded the order which had restricted him.

His second restriction was from 1931 to 1933. Around that time a Friar Minor was due to arrive. He was a superior in his Franciscan community and had been preaching in Apulia. He was coming here just for a visit—he was just passing by and was stopping to see Padre Pio. The people heard about this friar coming, even though we had kept it secret. They got upset and frightened, thinking that this stranger was coming here to remove Padre Pio. They came up to the friary in the middle of the night in protest. The door was locked, but they forced it open. They broke through the door to take the friar away. A big crowd surged through the cloister, and they were screaming: We want this, we want that!

I went down to meet them. I told them that what they thought was not true. They answered: "You are a liar." Then I raised my hands and said: "Out! Out! Everybody get out!" They obeyed me and retreated.

They made Padre Pio come to the window. That calmed the crowd down. To help quiet them, I let the chief of police get up on a soap box and speak to them; he convinced them and made them leave. For the rest of the night one of the carabinieri stayed to guard the friary as a precaution. After that everything quieted down.

The Holy See tried to keep the lid on everything. Then an inquiry came from Rome, and in June an order came that Padre Pio would be allowed to do only one thing: celebrate Mass. All other faculties—hearing Confessions and everything else—were taken away. He was forbidden to see anyone at all—no one. I think that was June 11. That morning his Mass lasted for two or three hours—not less than two hours. He celebrated Mass all by himself, except for a couple of boys from the seminary. Then when he offered Mass, if they couldn't come, he would celebrate all by himself.

In May I dreamed that Padre Pio was going to be released from these restrictions on July 5, the sixth Sunday after Pentecost. I went to Padre Pio and told him the dream. I asked him: "Is this true?" He said: "Let's hope that these flowers will blossom."

The dream came true. Pope Pius XI sent a visitator, a Capuchin named Pasetta. He came suddenly to the friary along with Bevilacqua. They related to Padre Pio what the Pope had said, and they returned to the Pope with what Padre Pio had said. After a while the Pope came to realize where the truth actually was and what the problems were. He released Padre Pio from his restrictions in July.

The Pope said to Archbishop Cucarolla, a Capuchin: "You Capuchins have a grand triumph. You must be very happy, because this is the first time that the Holy Office has ever withdrawn an order. The Holy Office has swallowed all of their own commands."

They released Padre Pio because they realized that they had made a mistake. The archbishop of Manfredonia [who had denounced Padre Pio to the Holy See as a fraud] was deposed [for reasons unrelated to Padre Pio]. He was defrocked and sent home.

[*Padre Pio's spirituality included a strong devotion to the Poor Souls in Purgatory. Padre Raffaele recalled an incident that involved much more than the mere devotion of Padre Pio's heart.*]

Do you know the story of the dead man? It happened around 1918 or 1919, around the time Padre Pio came to San Giovanni Rotondo. Assunta, the sister of Padre Paolino, had come to visit her brother. In the evening, since the hour was late and her room was far away, she occupied a small room in the guest quarters of the friary. After supper, Padre Paolino said to Padre Pio: "Let's go and say hello to Assunta in the guest quarters."

While they were visiting with her, Padre Pio became very drowsy and sat down next to the fireplace. It was November, and it was quite cold. Seeing Padre Pio so tired, Padre Paolino said to him: "We are going to pay a visit to the Blessed Sacrament. In the meanwhile, you stay here and rest, because you are so tired." Padre Pio agreed, and Paolino and his sister went into the church through the sacristy.

Before long Padre Pio fell into a light sleep. Suddenly he woke up. He opened his eyes and saw an old man bundled up in a heavy overcoat, warming his hands by the fire. He said to the old man: "Who are you? What are you doing here?" The old man replied: "I am so and so."

Padre Pio said: "What are you doing here?" He answered: "I am in Purgatory to atone for this and this."

Padre Pio said: "Well, I'm talking to you now, and we will not talk about this any more. Tomorrow morning I will offer a Mass for you and you will be liberated, but you—don't you come here any more."

He took the old man by the arm and walked outside with him as far as the tree [the famous tree in the piazza around which Padre Pio and his friends used to visit with each other]. Padre Pio said to the old man: "Don't come back here any more." He said goodbye to the old man, and the old man disappeared. Padre Pio returned to the friary alone.

When he reached the friary, he found the door locked. Remember that when Padre Pio had walked outside, the door remained locked, because when he came back, he found the door locked and bolted. So he rang the bell.

Padre Paolino opened the door and asked: "What are you doing outside? How did you get out here?"

Padre Pio answered: "I had to go to the bathroom." That was Padre Pio's first answer. Later Padre Pio explained what had really happened.

Padre Paolino said: "Don't hand me that story. It is not true, because the door was locked."

Padre Pio said: "No, no, the door was open."

Paolino said: "No, the door was locked." The debate went back and forth.

After a few days Padre Pio said: "I said that the door was open because I didn't want to explain what really happened." So it is clear that Padre Pio went outside through the closed door, and he was trying to come in with the door closed.

For several days Padre Pio did not look well. He was very pensive and sad and pale. Padre Paolino asked him several times: "What happened that night? Don't you feel well? Are you sick?" At first Padre Pio would not say anything. Finally he told Paolino what had actually happened concerning the old man.

The next day Padre Pio sent Paolino to the city hall to find out about this old man who had died—to learn his name and when and where he had died. They told him: "Yes, there was an old man who had died at the friary. He was burned alive in room number 4. His name was something like Preconci. At that time the friary was a home for the poor. The poor used room number 4. This man used to smoke a lot in bed. One night in 1886 this man set his bed on fire and was burned alive." I have no doubt that Padre Pio had spoken to this dead man from San Giovanni Rotondo. That is one story.

Now I want to tell you another story that happened in the church. Every evening after supper all the friars used to come together for a common recreation, and Padre Pio would go with them. Then Padre Pio would go to the oratory and pray by himself.

One evening as Padre Pio was all by himself praying in the oratory, he heard a noise in the church. He thought: "It must be the students—the boys who are straightening things up in the church." So he didn't pay any further attention to the incident.

There were candles all around the altar. You would have to use a ladder to get to them. As Padre Pio was praying, he heard a noise like—vroom—everything came crashing down. He got up from where he was and went to the Communion rail. He saw a young man dressed as a friar. The man was kneeling down. Padre Pio went up to him and said in a loud voice: "Eh, who are you?"

The young man said: "I am a Capuchin novice, and I am from Purgatory, doing penance for the lack of diligence in my work in the church."

Padre Pio said: "Well, then! This is a fine way to make reparation—breaking up all the candles! Now listen to me. Go away, and don't you come here any more. Tomorrow my Mass will be for you. In this way you will be liberated. Never come back." The novice thanked him, and Padre Pio left the church. When Padre Pio realized that he had been speaking to a dead man, a cold shiver ran up and down his spine.

While this was happening, Padre Emanuele was passing by. He said to Padre Pio: "Did you talk with a dead man? I was standing near the Communion rail and I realized that you were talking with a dead man. I got so scared I ran out. I went to get help." He returned with Padre Paolino.

Padre Pio was shaking. He said: "I'm cold, I'm cold." Paolino asked him what had happened. He answered: "I was talking with a dead man."

After about twenty minutes he said to Emanuele: "Get a candle and come with me."

"Where are we going?"

"Come!" They went into the church to the main altar. Padre Pio said: "Jump up on the altar."

He did. Then he asked: "Now what do you want me to do?"

Padre Pio said: "Look behind the altar. Are there any broken candles there?" At the time the altar had a picture of St. Michael on it. He said: "Look under the picture of St. Michael behind the altar, and see if there are any broken candles."

Emanuele looked and said: "Yes. There are some large candles here. They are all broken. Now what else?"

Padre Pio said: "Now come down. That's enough. No more. Let's get out of here." And they walked out of the church.

17. Padre Clemente da Santa Maria in Punta, Capuchin Alessandria

For a religious (that is, a member of a religious community, such as the Capuchins) there is a double chain of command. First there is his own religious organization: his local minister, his Minister Provincial, and his Minister General. Then there is the ecclesiastical organization: his local bishop (who has jurisdiction only in matters touching his ministry but not in matters which are strictly internal to the religious community, such as bookkeeping and prayer life). Finally there is the Holy See, with its numerous congregations, and of course, the Pope.

Padre Clemente had the unique advantage of holding positions in both echelons: religious and ecclesiastical. As a Capuchin he was a definitor (councilor) on both the international and Provincial levels. Also he was a consultor for three Vatican congregations: the Congregation for Religious, the Holy Office (now called the Congregation for the Doctrine of the Faith), and the Congregation for the Causes of Saints. His work in all these capacities brought him in close touch with Padre Pio. Perhaps even more significantly, the turbulence of the times to which I alluded in my previous interview with Padre Raffaele was the very occasion of some of Padre Clemente's contacts with Padre Pio.—JS

* * *

Just before I arrived, a rumor was going around that people in the Home for the Relief of Suffering wanted to take Padre Pio away from the friary and bring him to the hospital and have him move in. These people wanted him to abandon the friary and live in the Casa. This was in 1962, during the pontificate of Pope John XXIII.

One of the Fathers, to see what was behind the rumor, came up with the idea of installing some microphones in the rooms where Padre Pio would meet the people. He did this in good faith, moved by the fear of losing Padre Pio. This story of the microphones immediately reached Rome and was heard at the Holy Office. They decided to send Bishop Macari as an apostolic visitor.

The apostolic visitor saw what was going on and notified the Holy See as to the points on which he wanted to put restrictions. And usually when the Holy See sends their own representative, they do what their representative tells them. He presented all kinds of rules and regulations which greatly restricted Padre Pio's activities to the extent that every day the schedule for Padre Pio's Mass had to be changed. One day his Mass would be at five, the next day at five-thirty, then six, and so forth. Bishop Macari did not want any regularity in this matter. That was the order from the Holy See.

Then Bishop Macari gave another order. When Padre Pio came out of his confessional, he was not to look around or talk to anyone. And this is interesting: when Padre Pio was under this pressure and under these strict orders, he complied peaceably with everything he was told. He never complained.

In one of these pastoral visits to Padre Pio, his superior asked him what he wanted. Padre Pio answered: "I want only to be treated exactly as any other Capuchin here, nothing more or less."

On September 8, 1963, after the death of Pope John XXIII, I was sent by Pope Paul VI to Foggia [the headquarters of the Province which included San Giovanni Rotondo] as apostolic visitor. At that time San Giovanni Rotondo depended directly on the Holy Office. [This arrangement was rare. Ordinarily each friary depends directly on the Provincial Superior, not on the Vatican.]

Let me put it this way. I was the superior of the whole Capuchin Province. But as long as the Province depended on the Holy See, San Giovanni Rotondo and Padre Pio were subject to the Holy Office. Therefore, I had two [Vatican] congregations upon which I depended as visitor: the Congregation for Religious, and the Holy Office.

This is why I was sent: because the person before me had imposed such restrictions. Pope Paul VI gave me this order: "Liberate Padre Pio from those restrictions." I had to make it easy for Padre Pio to conduct his ministry in peace, without any restrictions. One of the things that the Pope told me was that I had to make the work of Padre Pio easy as a condition necessary for his apostolate.

Pope Paul VI was aware of the crisis in the friary. All their students and novices had been sent to another Province. The Definitors and Provincial had been dismissed. Therefore, my work was two-fold: to release Padre Pio from his restrictions and to restore normalcy to the Province.

When I got there, I immediately took away the restriction on the irregular schedule of his Mass; he could say Mass at any time he wanted. I took away the restriction of what he could do or not do after Confession. I told him that after he heard Confessions he could talk with anyone he wanted.

I also took away the restriction pertaining to the sacristy behind the little church. Now he could receive anyone he wanted and talk to anyone he wanted. So when he would come out of the confessional, he would stop and talk with the people on his way back to the sacristy. I did everything that the Pope told me to make his life easier. I removed the sacristy from the cloister so that he could receive people any time he wanted, including women. I sent a report to the Pope, and I told him what I had done. I said: "If this man is free to hear Confessions, he should be free to do everything else."

The Pope himself came to that same conclusion: that the restrictions should be lifted. He drew a line. He said: "You of the Holy Office—leave this Father free to confess. Don't deny him permission to confess. Don't confine him like a criminal. Give him the permission to hear Confessions." The Pope said: "I can't see why you have to forbid him from hearing Confessions."

The restrictions on Padre Pio at the time of Pope John XXIII and Pius XI had been imposed for similar reasons. Popes are men like ourselves; a lot depends on who is around them, like with

President Nixon and Vietnam. Even though they are Popes and can issue any order they want, their conduct really depends on their counselors who surround them. The Popes are obliged to follow certain patterns.

There were those who did not believe in Padre Pio's holiness. Pope John XXIII listened to those counselors, and because of them he imposed the rigid restrictions. There were other incidents that happened, but I cannot talk about them now—it would be improper for me to talk about them.

[*I asked Padre Clemente if Pope Pius XII had dispensed Padre Pio from his vow of poverty, as some writers have claimed.*]

No. Pope Pius XII granted Padre Pio the faculty to administer the entire Home for the Relief of Suffering. Just like any other individual religious, Padre Pio had a vow of poverty. It is not true, as is written in newspapers, that the Pope dispensed Padre Pio from the vow; he was not dispensed from the vow. The Pope said: "You can do everything with the total income of the hospital."

In that way Padre Pio could say: "With the money I can pay a doctor or a professor or build another building." Therefore, Padre Pio was always under the vow of poverty, and at the same time he could dispose of hospital funds and goods as he saw fit. The only suspension from the vow of poverty pertained to the hospital.

[*The Church today is heir to two millennia of experience concerning saints and claims that people are saints. I considered my interview with Padre Clemente, therefore, as a unique opportunity to ask again the same question I had asked several others: Do you have any comment on the article in the American Medical Association journal alleging that Padre Pio's stigmata might have been attributed to autosuggestion stemming from hysteria?*]

Before my assignment to Foggia, I was consultor for the Vatican congregation which deals with the beatification of saints. I investigated the stigmata and other claims. Authors whom I studied all talked about hysteria. But when these same authors spoke about Padre Pio, they spoke in a positive sense, that is, they spoke about the stigmata, but they did not conclude that the stigmata were the result of hysteria. They could have said that his stigmata were the fruit of hysteria, but instead they didn't say anything. For other people, they pronounced for hysteria. For these authors not to pronounce something is a positive reason for us to accept it.

We didn't see anything to indicate hysteria in Padre Pio. There are signs by which you can tell if a person is hysterical. But in him there were no signs. You have to have proof if you say that someone is hysterical, and not just say so. What proof did the author of that article have?

I'd say to these people: "Give me the reasons and the proofs which you have which indicate that Padre Pio was hysterical. Give me the proof! I can't prove falsity if you don't know the truth." An author can allege that Padre Pio was hysterical, but I say no, he was not. I don't know any other way to answer you better than this: go to New York and say to that author: "Tell me why you say that Padre Pio was hysterical. We want to know why you say that." We should not close our eyes and let it go. But we have to know why people say that Padre Pio was hysterical, and then we can answer them. All of this refers to the man himself: Padre Pio. And we have to defend his cause.

He behaved like any normal person. He was just like any normal man—he did what a normal person does. Sometimes he talked seriously, sometimes he told little jokes, then he laughed—just like any normal person.

Somebody might say that things happened in Padre Pio's life that were not normal. For example, he ate so little—so little that I tried to get him to eat a little more. He would answer: "I just can't eat any more."

There were times when he had very high fevers. Quite often Padre Pio had a fever that exceeded forty degrees centigrade [104 fahrenheit]. The heat broke the thermometer. This is something that doesn't happen often to many people. Perhaps also there were things that Padre Pio could see at a distance. Of course you can find that phenomenon among people everywhere, but this doesn't mean that these people are hysterical.

[*Shortly before Padre Pio died he wrote a letter to Pope Paul VI, thanking him for and professing complete obedience to his encyclical* Humanae vitae. *What a consolation Padre Pio's letter must have been to the Pope, when a hue and cry rose up around the world against the encyclical. I asked Padre Clemente what his own role was in Padre Pio's letter.*]

I'll explain how that letter came about. I was a General Definitor (councilor to our Minister General in Rome). The General Chapter was going to be received in an audience by Pope Paul VI. I asked Padre Carmelo, the superior at San Giovanni Rotondo, to ask Padre Pio if he had anything in particular to say to the Pope. I'd take it with me personally.

Padre Pio spoke verbally, and Padre Carmelo wrote the letter. Padre Carmelo realized that Padre Pio was over eighty years old, and he knew the mind of Padre Pio. Padre Pio said: "Tell the Pope this and this." Padre Pio read it and signed it.

Before we had the audience with the Pope, Padre Pio died. I took the letter to the secretary of state in the Vatican. Some days later it was published in the newspaper *L'Osservatore Romano* [the semi-official newspaper of the Vatican]. The letter was very important because it shows that Padre Pio was consistently obedient to his superiors. What Padre Pio said in the letter was the stand which he took constantly. When he found penitents not following this rule, he dismissed them. He was always very obedient to the Pope.

He used to say to priests: "Don't act the way I do. You don't have to behave the way I behave. But follow the rules of morality of the Church and you won't have to send people away without a reason." The reason why he would send them away was to make them think it over and repent and confess. These people did come back repentant, and they confessed. I spoke with them, and they were changed persons when they came back. What I mean to say is that his method of sending them away was perhaps an instrument that God inspired him to use.

Padre Pio lives in the memory of those who have met him. Now after his death, people who have never met him can read what has been written about him, and they can see his pictures. But most of all, souls who are searching for something can read the book that has just come out: *The Letters*. Reading the *Letters* and the biographies puts a person in contact with the soul of Padre Pio, with the reputation of Padre Pio, and with the personality of Padre Pio.

I think people remember this great man because he was a great saint. He lived the life of a saint. What he did during his life touches all nations. I think this world needs Padre Pio.

18. Padre Aurelio, Capuchin
San Giovanni Rotondo

Few people had the privilege of knowing Padre Pio as long as Padre Aurelio knew him, from 1916 to 1968. Padre Aurelio was a seminarian in the Scuola Media, the equivalent of our junior high school, when Padre Pio was spiritual director. I asked him to reminisce about Padre Pio's days as a young priest.—JS

* * *

Padre Pio was very open, very generous. I was a student at the seminary from 1916 to 1918; he was the director of the boys. Our classes with him were not classes in the real sense of that word—he was not an official teacher. He gave some classes and taught us religion, but only as a substitute. Sometimes he taught history, but he didn't have any background for teaching. The classes were superficial, because Padre Pio didn't know how to teach. Sometimes he would skip an examination. He would let everything go, and he would let us get away with everything. He was like a little bird in the class. He would let us do whatever we wanted. He was not a severe judge.

He used to give us kids a conference every Saturday. Occasionally he would make some little points about his vocation. He would talk to us about his own vocation and make us fall in love with his Capuchin vocation and follow him. He used to tell us that as a boy he knew he had a vocation because he liked to pray.

He liked short little prayers. When Padre Pio himself was a boy, he would go off by himself, apart from the other boys while they were playing and not let anyone else see him. He would go to Mass when the other boys wouldn't. All this shaped his vocation as a Capuchin Franciscan.

He wrote out his conferences and read them every time. He

would stand at a small lectern and read his conferences, which lasted about twenty minutes, not more. They were beautiful—they would encourage us to strengthen and purify our vocation. His conferences have been lost. That's unfortunate, because they were very beautiful.

He gave us his last conference after he received the stigmata [September 20, 1918]. Perhaps it was on that very day. I was there, but I didn't see anything of the stigmata. As he read his conference, he had a mantle over his shoulders, and he would wrap his hands in the ends of the mantle. We didn't notice anything that everyone else was talking about—the stigmata, the stigmata. We didn't see anything. No one saw anything. But when I went to his room, I saw his bed wet with blood. That was a couple of days after he received the stigmata.

He was very paternal and understanding. There was only one exception: he was very strict when we boys would talk in church. That is the only thing he couldn't stand, but he would close his eyes to everything else, always. He didn't censure us for anything else.

We were impressed by his humanity, even more than by his holiness. He understood us, he had compassion, and he was especially sympathetic. After we were ordained and lived with him as priests, he was holy, yes, but this attraction as far as we were concerned was relative, and we looked on it superficially. We set it aside. But we would go to him because in him we found sympathy, charity and understanding.

He had some sort of an attraction, a charm. I can affirm this, because one day I received a very serious punishment for something I didn't do. I am embarrassed to have to say this, but I was confined to my room. Every night he would come to my room and sit on my bed and stay until one or two o'clock in the morning to comfort me and talk to me. He'd console me because I was depressed over the punishment. He would even go against the rules, because the rule allowed him to stay with us only till midnight. He would leave my room when he would remember that Padre Paolino, the superior, would yell at him if he would find him in my room. They also reprimanded him if it was after one o'clock in the morning—he could stay with us till midnight but not later. He was like a father.

During World War I we had nothing to eat, so the boys used to steal bread and other things so that we could have something to eat. Padre Pio knew of it—he didn't condone it, but he let it go without making an issue of it. He didn't say: "Go and steal," but he knew what we were doing, and he didn't say anything about it.

I'd say that Padre Pio's holiness consisted precisely in his humility. He would share everything and not keep anything for himself. We used to go to the dining room, and he would go with us. Some of the boys got really angry and fought over the food, because there wasn't enough food for us. Padre Pio didn't eat anything. He would give everything away.

He used to give everything to the boys. Whatever he had, he used to give to us. In his room he had some candy and fruit. He would take us to his room and let us eat it. After we became priests, he would take us to his room and say: "Let the others eat, because we have so many things here." But when we were kids, he would treat us like a mama.

He also had a fine sense of humor. One day in 1917 we played a practical joke on the people in town. We had something like a kite, but it was very, very big. Underneath it we put a little bomb, and a little lamp attached to it. It really scared the people of the town. We had a long rope tied to the end of the kite. For about an hour we flew the kite all around the sky. The people saw it and were terrified. Padre Pio and the chief of police knew about it, but they let us enjoy the joke.

[*I asked Padre Aurelio to share with me his most vivid recollection of Padre Pio.*]

It is very personal. It was something when I was a young boy at the Scuola Media. We used to go to Padre Pio every night for a blessing. After the students would receive his blessing, if they had been delinquent during the day they would go back to him for a special blessing. That irritated me.

I was the "chief" of the boys. One day I yelled at one of them,

Nardello, the nephew of Padre Benedetto, the Provincial. I had great respect for him, but he was a troublemaker. I said to him: "You have been a scoundrel. You have to go back to Padre Pio by yourself and get his blessing."

He answered me: "I already got his blessing. The case is closed."

I said: "Aren't you ashamed of yourself?" I thought it was my duty to yell at this kid.

Padre Pio was inside and heard our voices. He came out and said: "Who is shouting?"

The boys answered: "It's the chief. He's the one doing the shouting."

Padre Pio said to me: "Is this the way to give good example?"

Every night Padre Pio used to go around and stop in the rooms where the boys slept, and he would close their doors. This evening he came near my bed and said: "Get ready for bed like everyone else. Do you want me to bless you?"

I said: "Why not!"

He asked me twice: "Aureliuccio [my dear little Aurelio], do you want me to close your door?"

I said: "Why wouldn't you want to close my door?"

He said: "All right, I'll close your door for the night." He went around to each room and came back to my room. He said "I want you to mend your ways," and he said I would soon be sorry for my caprice.

That night someone came to my room. Surely this is very personal. I was sitting in my underwear on my bed. This visitor was a monster; I was petrified. This person was like a shadow whose breath smelled terrible. I thought that it was a hallucination. But later Padre Pio explained that it wasn't a hallucination.

I resisted this person until twelve-thirty. He broke a little glass statue of the Blessed Mother which I had on my night table. He threw it onto the floor, and it shattered. I was petrified. I couldn't move.

In the morning I got out of bed, and still in my underwear I

knocked on door number five, Padre Pio's room. He said: "Eh?"
I said: "I want to go away. I want to go home. I think I'm going to die because I saw the devil. I saw the devil!"

Padre Pio said: "Don't worry. Come and sleep in my bed." He put me to sleep in his own bed. He himself walked up and down the corridor, because it was almost time for the other boys to get up.

At eight o'clock in the morning he woke me up. I said again: "I don't want to stay, because I have seen the devil."

Padre Pio said to me: "That was the proof that the Lord wanted to give you. But thank God you didn't see him like he really is. You didn't come to get a blessing from me. So you see what can happen to you at night if you don't come for my blessing." He said: "From now on, before you go to bed, I'll bless you every night, even from far away."

That is the story which I remember. It really happened. I swear to it. Padre Pio never let me forget this incident. From then on I'd never sleep in that room. It is now Father Guardian's room.

The dormitory for eight of us boys is now the room used for the archives. Padre Pio slept with us in this dormitory. His bed was near the window. Around his bed he had a curtain with a heavy iron rod which held the curtain. If you could only have seen what happened one night!

We boys were always talking in the dormitory. Padre Pio could never keep us quiet. So one night he said to us: "Please, don't let the superior have to tell me again to keep the silence. Please be quiet. Don't make me look bad. Don't say a single word. Good night."

We said: "Okay, we won't talk. We won't do anything."

In the morning when we got up, we saw Padre Pio's bed turned completely upside down and twisted. Also, the curtain and the iron curtain rod were all twisted up like a piece of curly hair. The rod was as thick as your finger, but the whole length of the rod was all twisted and turned. We were really scared.

Padre Pio came along, and we asked him what had happened. He said: "It's incredible. When I finally get a promise out of you to keep the silence, along comes Barbablu [a name Padre Pio used to refer to the devil] and messes up everything." He added: "Believe me, it's nothing. Don't make a big deal of it." He said that one of the workers had twisted up the iron bar. Later it was straightened out and put back in its place.

19. Padre Eusebio, Capuchin Campobasso

Padre Eusebio lived with Padre Pio for five years. When Padre Pio was old and weak, Padre Eusebio was one of the few friars privileged to take care of his personal needs.—JS

* * *

How can I express my experiences of five years in a few words. I was very, very close to Padre Pio. I took care of his room and his person. Before coming to San Giovanni Rotondo, I didn't believe in him. My skepticism was not about his stigmata but about his sanctity. (I do not identify the stigmata with sanctity.) In the beginning I wasn't sure about his holiness. At that time he was under restrictions, and you would hear so many things. Many people were against him, and I didn't know whom to believe. I don't agree a priori with other people. I had to see for myself who Padre Pio was.

I had been in England. When I returned to Italy, Father Provincial sent me to San Giovanni Rotondo. When I got there, I tried to look at Padre Pio and see if it was true or not that he was really a holy man, so I conducted an experiment for myself—I tried to spy—to spy! It was not difficult for me to acquire an experience of what he was, especially in his prayer life and the times he read people's minds, and in the way he would answer their questions. Now, afterwards, I believe in everything. I am convinced that Padre Pio was an extraordinary man, really a holy man.

I did see the stigmata many, many times. I would be directly in front of him, and I could see his wounds very clearly. Also, many times I saw his hands bleeding through his gloves. There is no doubt about that, because I saw them. Every morning, in the washroom, and in his room where he used to wash, I found crusts there, because he cleaned his wounds in the morning. It was painful for him. He had to push the crusts aside and leave them somewhere.

I didn't measure it, but I don't believe that he lost a pint or a half pint of blood every day, at least when I was there. In the beginning, soon after he got the wounds in 1918, the blood was flowing—that is correct. But I never saw anything like that. I am referring to the period between 1960 and 1965. That's quite different from 1918. I'm talking about my own experience. Think about two or three or four handkerchiefs full of blood. Think of that. How much blood was that? You cannot measure it.

Nevertheless, there were occasions when he would lose very much blood. Sometimes I found the sheets of his bed covered with blood, and at those times he was compelled to renew his bandages twice a day, especially the bandage on the wound of his heart.

I must tell you something about the wound of his heart. One day Padre Pio fell down. He had been pushed by the devil— something like that. When we found him, he was really covered by blood. I was there, and I saw him. He had not fallen out of bed, although that is what he told us. That was at the time when there was a woman there who was possessed by the devil. The devil spoke through her and said that he himself had pushed Padre Pio down.

The doctor was called to treat Padre Pio. I was the only priest who helped Padre Pio to change his undershirt on that occasion. It was then that I saw the wound of his side. It was really marvelous. The long part of the wound of his heart, which was horizontal, was about four inches long, as long as my little finger. Across that was a shorter one, about two or three inches long, crossing at an angle, left to right. It was not bloody; it was not bleeding; but it was an open wound.

I saw the photographs of his body that were taken [in rapid sequence] immediately after his death. First, in one picture, you could see the wound of his side. In another photograph it was smaller. In another, smaller. And in another—*nothing*!

[*I asked Padre Eusebio about Padre Pio's personality, with particular reference to the possibility of hysteria as a cause of the stigmata.*]

Many doctors visited Padre Pio precisely to see if he was hysterical. They concluded that he was not. I have a whole lecture on Padre Pio and the doctors, and I give their names. I could give you their names which perhaps would be unknown to you, but they are of the greatest importance to people who know Italian doctors. The best doctors of Italy were his friends. How could you imagine that the doctors could be Padre Pio's friends if they noticed something wrong with his mind? It was not only a few of them, but many, from the universities of Naples and Rome.

Another thing. There are some doctors who are not Catholics. They went to Padre Pio because they were impressed by his personality, not by his wounds or his holiness—no—but by his personality.

If a person is hysterical, he has to show some signs of hysteria. A hysterical person would be laughed at in the way he looks at you, in the words he uses, in the way he behaves or wants something. Padre Pio was perfectly normal. Also, if he had been hysterical, his wounds would be superficial and not have any depth. Nor would they have lasted very long—more than a few hours or a few days. Padre Pio's wounds perdured.

[*I asked Padre Eusebio what was the most striking phenomenon he had seen—possibly a miracle?*]

I have seen many things. My favorite reflection is how he lived: the kind of a life he lived. Not miracles or anything like that. You can find that in the lives of all the saints. But Padre Pio, you should have lived with him from early in the morning till late at night. You would see the kind of life he lived.

He would get up very early in the morning, clean his wounds and start to say the rosary and pray and meditate. Afterwards Mass. At the end of his life his Mass was short—only a half hour. But don't forget that when he was stronger, his Mass used to last an hour or an hour and a half or two hours.

After that, he stayed for many hours and heard Confessions. I myself also have spent many hours in the confessional, but people came to me just for Confession. People would go to him not only for Confession but with every kind of question you could imagine: should I enter the hospital, should I have an operation, should I leave this job and take another? He always had presence of mind to give each person an answer—to each one of them. I know how difficult it is to imagine this, because a confessor must keep his mind only on each individual penitent.

After hearing Confessions, he would go upstairs. Along the stairs and along the corridor were people after him with more questions, always after him for something. I know that at times he didn't give any answer, but sometimes he used to answer each question: "Yes—no—leave this one—take another one—no—don't go there." How could he tell? If I should speak like that, you would think that I am a madman.

Another thing: the same question made by different people sometimes got a different answer. This is very important. It means that something was good for you but not good for the other party. He didn't say: "Please let me think about it." No! Bing, bing, bing, bing. He had the answer. How can you explain that? I'm not saying that Padre Pio was inspired by God all the time. I am saying that God was with Padre Pio all the time, to help him not make mistakes as I did. I have seen that.

When he ate, his food really was very, very poor. How could he live that way? He would eat a piece of macaroni and a tiny piece of fish. Nothing else. That was all the food he had for the entire day. Humanly speaking he had no other source of nourishment.

When he finally went to bed, he used to break his sleep to pray the rosary and to say ejaculations. He got up very early in the morning at one o'clock, at half past one, or at two o'clock. How much he prayed! The way he said Mass! The way he stayed with us! He would tell stories, and at the end of a story he would have a good word to convince us to be better in our spiritual life.

When I give lectures on Padre Pio, I seldom tell stories about him. Yes, people need stories, but if you fill them with stories, I don't think it is the best way to portray Padre Pio. He was a man who put the theology of the cross in a special way: why you have to suffer *to help God*, because God wants you to help Him to bring souls to Him. Not to go against God because you suffer; you must accept it, because God is a Father who sees value in your suffering. It is difficult for us to express this theology.

I can see in Padre Pio something that has helped me. He has made my life quite different. He was a priest in whom God was particularly alive: in his life, in his way of bringing people to God. I'm not talking just about his wounds. He was like a lamp to enlighten people and to bring them on the right path to God. There is much that I can say about this, but it can't be said in a few minutes. I lecture on why Padre Pio suffered.

20. Mrs. Aurelio Montalto
San Giovanni Rotondo

*Mr. and Mrs. Montalto are owners of and operators of the Albergo
Vittorio, a modern hotel near the friary in San Giovanni Rotondo.—JS*

* * *

We first came to San Giovanni Rotondo out of curiosity. We
had been visiting relatives, and although we were in a hurry to
return home, I stopped in a book store and bought a book on
Padre Pio. The book impressed me a lot, and I felt the need to
meet Padre Pio personally.

We came, all six of us, from Bolzano. When we attended his
Mass, it was like a little piece of heaven. After Mass we saw Padre
Pio at a distance, and his smile was like sunshine. At home we
could talk about nothing but Padre Pio. I felt that we just had to
go back. I thought: I must kiss his hand and thank him for
everything. So we returned, although I was awaiting the birth of
our baby. I wanted to have the baby at the Home for the Relief of
Suffering [Padre Pio's hospital]. I asked my doctor if I could
make the trip. He answered: "Absolutely not. The baby might be
born on the train."

In spite of his warning, I decided to leave right away, but I was
extremely tired from the housework and packing. I could not sit
comfortably in the train. By the time we reached the third station,
I said to myself: Padre Pio, how can I get down there like this, if I
am already so exhausted? You have to help me now. Otherwise I
can't go on. From that moment on, I felt completely comfortable,
and I lay down and slept.

In San Giovanni Rotondo, I waited for the birth of the baby, but
nothing happened. Christmas Day arrived, then Saint Stephen's
day, then the twenty-eighth. Again I thought: What could have
happened? So my husband reminded Padre Pio that we had

come to give birth to our child, that my mother was back home and not feeling well, and the little children needed us. Padre Pio said: "Don't let it worry you. The main thing is that everything goes well."

Finally, on January 3, about seven-thirty in the evening, my labor pains began. I walked to the hospital, and at nine the baby was born. My husband was in the hall. He smelled the scent of violets when the baby was born. As I was delivering, I prayed to Padre Pio and I saw him standing next to me. We named our baby Maria Pia Francesca.

While we were in San Giovanni Rotondo, my husband wanted to make a general Confession to Padre Pio, so he wrote everything down. He thought: I can read it in the confessional. Padre Pio didn't even let him talk. He told my husband everything that he had written down—in the right sequence!

After that visit we frequently visited Padre Pio, and then we moved here with our four children. They have all received their first Holy Communion from him.

We can say that Padre Pio was our family doctor. One of my brother's children was diagnosed as having a terminal illness. Her lungs were completely congested. She was cured by Padre Pio. Another daughter, a little baby of three weeks, was afflicted with a very serious disease of the bones. She too was cured by Padre Pio. This is how it is with everything—Padre Pio takes care of people.

At our hotel we met a blind girl from Iringen Kaiserstuhl. She had been in terrible spiritual turmoil; she was completely drawn into herself. She told me: "All I do is cry and cry and cry."

I said: "Why don't you go to Confession and talk to a priest? He can help you a lot." She said that she hadn't been to Confession for thirty-five years. With my help she made her Confession not to Padre Pio but to a German-speaking priest here. She was still physically blind.

One day she got out of the bus near the church and immediately thought of Padre Pio. From that moment she was able to see. She discarded the arm band that blind people wear, then the glasses, then her cane. Now she walks without any help. Her pension for the blind was discontinued. A countess named Richter has put the documentation together on the girl's story and has submitted it to the Capuchins.

I would like to tell you also of my husband's brother. He had never met Padre Pio. Then Padre Pio died. While his body was being waked in the church, my brother-in-law, who was not a believer in very much, tried to enter the church, but the door was closed before he could enter. He came back to stay with us. He was very disappointed. He told us: "Everybody talks about Padre Pio, but I don't believe what they say. I don't see anything, and I don't feel anything."

He went back to the church the next day, and for the next several days, and sat in the third pew from the back. He just sat still and looked around. Then one day he felt a tap on the shoulder and heard a rough voice. He turned around but nobody was there. He got scared, and he thought: Oh, that's nothing—it's only my imagination.

Still, he got up and went to the last bench. He sat there and looked and looked, and again he felt someone shaking his shoulder, and he heard the same rough voice. He turned around again but he didn't see anyone. He was bathed in perspiration.

Then my husband came along and said to him: "I'm driving to the village. Come along."

His brother said: "You know, I'm completely covered with perspiration. I have to tell you something." Then he told my husband everything. My husband didn't say a word. My brother-in-law said: "How does a person go about making a Confession?" He had never gone to Confession. He asked: "Where does he go and what must he say?" My husband explained everything. The next day he went to Confession and Communion.

That night he dreamed that Padre Pio came, holding a rosary in front of him and showed him how to pray. In his room he smelled the scent of incense. My brother-in-law became a convert and was really very happy with everything.

My own brother knew Padre Pio. After Padre Pio's death, he

told me: "You know, Martha, it's different now that Padre Pio isn't here. Before when Padre Pio was here . . . "

I interrupted him: "Ask Padre Pio for a sign."

The next day he went to the church and said: "Padre Pio, give me a sign that I can know that you know that I am here."

For the past four years my brother had been suffering from bad feet. His condition was incurable. He could not walk without a cane, not even for a few steps. That was very difficult, because the bones were rubbing and were exposed.

One evening all of us were together in the crypt [beneath the church, where Padre Pio is buried]. A Capuchin friar came and clapped his hands to give a signal for everyone to leave. We were the last ones.

We left the church and walked across the piazza. Suddenly my brother said: "Where did I leave my cane?"

I said: "Where were we just a moment ago?"

"In the church, at the crypt."

"Maybe you left it there."

He said: "I'll get it."

I said: "But the door is locked. We cannot get it now."

He said: "Well, I have come so far, and now I'm going to continue on."

The road leading down from the friary is very rough. I said: "Tomorrow morning Aurelio will accompany you up to the church."

At six o'clock the next morning my brother was already at the church. He never went back to get his cane. He left it there. He was completely cured.

I could tell you of many cases of people who have never met Padre Pio but have received wonderful graces in their prayers. Many conversions have happened after his death. I could tell you so much about Padre Pio—I could talk all day.

Personally I have no doubts. For me, Padre Pio is the best friend a person can have, next to Our Lord. He is very dear to Our Lord. His life was nothing but suffering, and Our Lord can grant him everything through his prayer—everything!

21. Martha Gemsch
San Giovanni Rotondo

Miss Martha Gemsch is another of the "old guard" in San Giovanni Rotondo. She knew Padre Pio personally and considered him her Spiritual Father. Through this interview I achieved what I was anxious to learn: precisely how Padre Pio guided lay men and women through their spiritual life. —JS

* * *

Padre Pio gave us so many ideas on how to pray. He was capable of entering our minds without being present. He never spoke a lot—he just made it understood through his capacity to work in our souls and in our minds. He prayed for us and got the graces from the Lord for us. That was his way of guiding us. The more we wanted to go ahead, the more graces we got. So when Padre Pio got the graces for us, we went ahead by ourselves without him having to explain much about it.

To explain it might be different for every soul. You can never say: "This is the way for you and for everyone." Every soul has its own way. He just got the graces from God for us to get the necessary light and the necessary strength to go on our way. He might have had rules in the past, but for us he didn't have any. He only inspired us from above, and he gave us the necessary graces to get ahead.

He spoke very often of the presence of God—in our heart and around us: "The kingdom of heaven is in you." He wanted us to study and to discover how to live in the presence of God. In the beginning you don't experience this. You have to go through the whole desert of your soul. It's not an easy thing.

He wanted us to get up early in the morning to pray and meditate. In the early hours of the day you meditate better than during the daytime. If you pray the rosary well, it's not hard to learn how to pray. In fact, he never suggested anything more to me.

He never allowed you to be bound to him. He always let you be free, with freedom of thought, without allowing any strings to remain to bind you to him. Never. Really, he didn't want you to depend on him, to be attached to him.

In this way he was directing us from above. He still does that now. I never feel a great difference between his life on this earth and now when he is dead. He had many ways of inspiring people even without their having met him. I wrote to a Benedictine priest in the Himalayas, in India. He wrote back and said that he seemed to have known Padre Pio without ever having met him once. Padre Pio worked everywhere.

My sister Lisa was an X-ray technician and wanted to bring the new methods to the missions of India. Padre Pio told her not to go, but she went all the same. Later on Padre Pio said to a mutual friend: "Is she going to go away?"

She went to Dar es Salaam. As they drove along, the driver lost control of the car and it went off the road. The door flew open and she fell out. We don't know if the car rolled over on her, but she smashed her leg. She was taken to the hospital and died the following morning. I heard of Lisa's death only after two days.

The day she died was the first day Padre Pio had returned to hear Confessions after a rather long illness. We were all in the big church, which had just been opened. When Padre Pio came in, he went to the little church to hear Confessions, and everybody followed him. But his face was very dark. I thought: How strange his face is today.

Then he shouted at us: "What are you waiting for? Go to the Blessed Sacrament." He looked straight at me because I was sitting in front of him, and he shouted again at me: "Why are you waiting here? Go to the Blessed Sacrament and pray there." Then he went into the confessional.

Padre Pellegrino was there, so I asked him: "What did he say? Did he say that I must leave and must go to the big church?" He answered me: "Yes, he said so."

I felt very strange, but when he left the confessional at 9:00 o'clock as usual, I was there to kiss his hand. He turned away from us. I thought that was very strange—after all the prayers we offered for his health. Then he left us. But then I understood. Lisa had died at the same time Padre Pio had that very dark face. In the hospital where she died, there were some nuns whom we knew. One of them came out of the room where my sister was and said: "Padre Pio was here. Padre Pio said to us: 'I feel so sorry about it, but I was here to assist her.' " The doctor said that she died with a smile on her face, although she was all alone in India.

22. Don Lino Tozzi
San Marino

Legion seems to be the number of people whom Padre Pio guided successfully in their choice of a vocation, often contrary to all apparent odds. For this reason I have included my interview with Don Lino Tozzi, a diocesan priest from the independent vest-pocket republic (23 square miles!) of San Marino. It can stand, I believe, as typical of many, many similar instances. —JS

* * *

I first met Padre Pio when I was a university student, twenty-two years old. On this occasion we didn't even talk about a vocation. After I graduated I taught bookkeeping in Milan for four years. Then in 1964, when I was twenty-six, I entered the seminary. It was a year of crisis, because I wasn't sure that my vocation to the priesthood would allow me to go out into the world and do good for people.

My parents, grandparents, uncles, and everyone else always put obstacles in my path. I was not the serene type of person they imagined as a pastor of a quiet little church. I was too lively, so they thought. I was not cut out for the priesthood. Also, I was an only child. Even my bishop had other plans for me. He was pressuring me to accept a career in the diplomatic corps.

Another priest named Padre Pio, a Minim of the Order of St. Francis of Paola, advised me to visit Padre Pio, with whom I was already in correspondence. I went to San Giovanni Rotondo (this was my second visit) and mentioned to him that in Rimini there was another Padre Pio, and I mentioned his family name: della Piane. Literally it means "from the flatlands."

Jokingly, Padre Pio corrected me. He said: *"Non piane, ma dalle vette"* ("not from the flatlands, but from the heights"), because the two priests had the same lofty spiritual ideals. It seems that they had some kind of telepathic communication between themselves.

In the confessional I spoke about my disappointment and uncertainty, and about my fitness for the priesthood. At the end of the Confession, Padre Pio put his hand on my shoulder and said: "Continue in your studies for the priesthood. This is your way."

In 1967, my third year in the seminary, I had another very bad crisis. This might have been due to the fact that I was still in the seminary while men younger than me were already saying Mass. Also, I wanted to get close to the other seminarians, but there was not much common ground. The younger seminarians lacked maturity. My impressions might have been all wrong, but they caused this crisis. As far as studies were concerned though, I was doing quite well.

My mother was well aware of my difficulties. She told me that she was going to visit Padre Pio, and that if he told me that I should continue, she would not put any more obstacles in my path. She went to San Giovanni Rotondo, and after waiting two days her turn finally came up for her to confess. She knelt down, but she couldn't say a word. He looked at her and said: "You are Lino's mother." She started to cry.

She made her Confession, and they started talking about me. Padre Pio told her not to put any obstacles in my path. He said that she should give me this message from him: I should go ahead because that was my vocation, I would have a lot of satisfaction in my work, I should not be discouraged, and I should visit him. He said that I would have the chance to do a lot of good. From that time on, my mother joined my cause. Then I myself visited Padre Pio. We spoke at length on my problems, and he was generous in his advice. There was no doubt that the priesthood was my vocation.

I was ordained in 1968. I am now working at the Centro Communitario para Tercer Mondo, in Puno, Peru, working with young people in depressed areas. As Padre Pio had assured me, the movement is coming along nicely. It has been written up in the press and has spread to other places. I am happy in this work, again as Padre Pio had promised, and I feel that we are accomplishing our ideals for a better world.

23. Mary Ingoldsby
San Giovanni Rotondo

Frequently people have told me—and I myself have experienced—that Padre Pio had an uncanny ability to bring people together. Mary Ingoldsby, Dublin-born, is a professional translator. She acknowledges quite definitely that it was the hand of Padre Pio that brought her to San Giovanni Rotondo to translate two volumes of his Letters.—JS

* * *

I was in Italy twenty years ago, working in the lay apostolate. I had met a lot of fanatical people in northern Italy who were giving trouble to Padre Pio and the friars, people who were going around sniffing the air and smelling his perfumes everywhere. I had no regard for Padre Pio at all. Then somebody brought me to San Giovanni Rotondo. The minute I got to Padre Pio's Mass and saw him, my whole idea changed. There was no doubt about it—it was like looking at Our Lord!

I returned to Rome to continue my work for the Second Vatican Council, and to direct a Holy Year Office for pilgrims in Rome. I read some of Padre Pio's letters which had been printed in the *Voice of Padre Pio*, and I felt that some of the translations were just terrible—it was a shame.

In the literature that I had picked up at San Giovanni Rotondo was the picture of an Irish group with a lady in the center. At twelve o'clock one day the phone rang, and an Irish voice said: "I'm in St. Peter's Square, and I want to come into your office. Our plane is leaving in a few minutes."

I told her to come, and in walked this lady who I thought was the lady in the middle of the photograph. I thought I was imagining things—that Padre Pio had got in on me. I registered her name: Mairead Doyle. This lady was the very same person!

In a hurry she gave me a lot of post cards to mail. They were all

of Padre Pio. I said: "Do you know anything of Padre Pio?"
She said: "I am a promotor for him in Dublin."
Immediately I said what I had on my mind: "What a pity the translations are so bad. It's a terrible shame to be doing that to Padre Pio."
She said: "They haven't got any translators." But I had no notion of coming to San Giovanni Rotondo—I have to earn my living. Our whole meeting lasted only five minutes, and I never thought any more about it.

About ten days later a girl in my office invited me to accompany her to San Giovanni Rotondo. I felt drawn to go with her. As I entered the office of the friary I met Father Joseph Pius. He said: "Hi, Mary! It's fine!" I remember those words.

I said: "What's fine?" It didn't seem to make sense to me.
He said: "It's fine about the letters, and about John McCaffrey."
I said: "What letters, and who is John McCaffrey?"

Father pelted upstairs to get a letter that had arrived a few days before from this spiritual son of Padre Pio, a man who had worked for Interpol and had been here many times. He had undertaken to look for a translator for the letters of Padre Pio. He had been looking and looking. Then he wrote to Father Joseph Pius: "I have found the translator. Her name is Mary Ingoldsby. She is in the Holy Year Office in Rome."

Father Joseph thought that we had been in touch, since John McCaffrey and I both come from Ireland, but I knew nothing about it. Mairead Doyle had told him about me, and he wrote to Father Joseph Pius.

I wrote to Mr. McCaffrey, and he immediately asked me to estimate the cost. He said: "I'll put up the money, but the letters must be properly translated."

I came here in July and started work on the *Letters*. The more I got into them, the more I loved Padre Pio. It is something extraordinary. You really get to know the man. You learn exactly what he is feeling. I felt as if I were on a retreat.

There are some letters that go on for pages and pages. He says in a letter to his spiritual director: "I am praying for you to the

God whom I have lost." He is convinced that he has lost God, that he is so bad. He has scruples about his past life and he thinks his Confessions were not good. He is tortured, and he cries out: "O God, whom I have lost!" It is the agony of the soul. It is terribly hard to translate.

Padre Benedetto reads that and comes back at him: "All this is meant by God. Just go ahead in absolute darkness. This is your mission: a mission of co-redemption."

I have caught onto those words: a mission of co-redemption. It is as if, according to Saint Paul, we fill up the sufferings of Christ [Colossians 1:24]. We fill up something, in our poor little way. We can make up what Christ has not yet suffered. In a huge way Padre Pio seems to be allowing Christ to suffer again in this century.

Padre Pio wasn't a literary genius. There is no literary style in the *Letters*, although at times he is like a poet, lyrical in the way he launches out into a description. On the whole there is no attempt to use style, but in his later letters he says things that are literary gems.

He was writing under obedience to his spiritual director. Many times he didn't want to. He nearly refused to describe these very deeply intimate things of his inner life—he asked to be dispensed from that. He said: "When we meet, I'll tell you." But the spiritual director insisted on his writing, and so we have these wonderful *Letters*.

In Rome I had been working in a new section of the Vatican which had been set up after the Council. To my mind, the people there were very superficial. They were talking, they were traveling all over the world, and going in a lot for sociology, psychology, anthropology, zoology, and all the rest of it, and the world was getting worse. It seemed to me that the prayer life, the life of suffering, like "Take up your cross and follow me" was outside of their work.

Then Padre Pio put me down here in San Giovanni Rotondo. I found that Padre Pio has all the answers to that. To my mind, he brings Christianity to our present consumer society, to city life particularly. Many others are not getting down to the real core of Christianity—to the harsh part of Christianity: "Take up your cross." Padre Pio brings you back to that. I think that is why he had the wounds of Christ. Padre Pio brings you back to this basic Christianity. He has a message for our world. He points to the Passion of Christ. I think my work for Padre Pio is the biggest thing I could possibly do for the Church.

24. Fra Modestino, Capuchin
San Giovanni Rotondo

The portineria, *the reception desk at the friary in San Giovanni Rotondo, is a crossroads. While Padre Pio was alive, it was the gauntlet that he had to run every time he went from the church to the friary. There his devotees lined up to see him, to kiss his hand, to fire a quick question at him, to ask his blessing. We may reasonably conjecture that the majority of visitors stopped at the front office. For most of the day the man on duty was the Capuchin Brother, Fra Modestino: unflappable, simple, smiling, solicitous, prayerful, busy, omniscient. But in the few minutes in which I sidetracked him from his multifarious duties, he showed me an image of Padre Pio which reconciled two apparently contradictory dimensions of Padre Pio: his suffering and his sense of humor. Without that balance, Padre Pio might have become a psychopath. With it, Padre Pio seemed to be just another one of the friars, to the consternation (as I learned) of some of the visitors.—JS*

* * *

Padre Pio was so human. He had a fine sense of humor. In 1944, twenty-five or thirty men were waiting to meet Padre Pio. As they waited for him, every one of them was anxious to kiss his hand. They were all staring at the door. They were saying to each other: "You introduce us." "No, *you* introduce us."

But when Padre Pio opened the door, they were all spellbound. They couldn't move. They couldn't say a word. Padre Pio came in, and with a big smile he said: *"Buon appetito!"* ("Good appetite!"). He closed the door behind himself and left.

As soon as the door closed, they were able to move again. One looked at the other, and they all said: "What happened? I couldn't move."

Another time Padre Pio was coming out of the sacristy to the church, and a woman came up to him and asked: "Where is the holy Father?"

Padre Pio answered her: "The Holy Father is in Rome." He continued to walk with her to the door. Padre Pio entered the friary, and the woman asked me: "Where is the holy Father?" I told her: "You were just talking to him."

Even with this sense of humor, Padre Pio was a man of suffering. It was very difficult for him to cough because of the wound in his side. I myself personally handled the undershirts which he wore. There was a cross of blood over the shoulder. Padre Placido testified to that wound on his shoulder. There were very dark bruises.

On March 5, 1967, Padre Pellegrino wiped Padre Pio's face of perspiration during Mass. But instead of the odor of sweat, the odor of blood came onto the handkerchiefs. Padre Pellegrino had to leave the altar, because he thought he would throw up. He saved eleven of those handkerchiefs and gave them to Padre Onorato to be saved. In January 1971, when they were to be placed in a plastic package for identification with the date and name, three of the handkerchiefs had blood on them, including one very heavily stained with blood. One was lightly stained, and the third reminded us of three tears of blood, each about the size of a quarter.

Padre Pio once said: "My God, how my eyes hurt me so badly. For three years I haven't been able to close my eyes, and I'm dying for sleep." Padre Pio offered this up to guide souls.

25. Pietruccio
San Giovanni Rotondo

What was his last name? I kept hearing of Pietruccio, a name I recognized as a diminutive form of Peter, but nobody seemed to know his last name. Later I learned it is Cugino. But the name Pietruccio alone was sufficient identification. Everybody knows "Pietruccio the blind man." He was born in 1913 and became blind at the age of twelve, when his family moved to San Giovanni Rotondo. As one of Padre Pio's most cherished spiritual sons, had he ever asked Padre Pio for a miracle? Pietruccio's casual comment startled me. Padre Pio asked him if he would like to see again. The very simple, childlike remarks of this blind man put two things in perspective for me: the relative importance (or unimportance) of physical eyesight to see the truest values in life, and the real Padre Pio—not a miracle-worker, but a Good Shepherd of souls.—JS

* * *

I never asked Padre Pio that I may get my eyesight back. But once he asked me: "Do you want to see again?"

I said to him: "No, Father. I don't want to. Only if it is good for my soul and for the welfare of other people that I see again will I accept that grace from Our Lady."

Padre Pio answered me: "You know very well that the eyes are the windows of our bodies. The dangers come always through our eyes."

I answered him: "Then I am happy to stay in this condition."

Many times Padre Pio said to me: "Good for you, Pietruccio, that you can't see the bad things of the world." And I said to him: "Father, I'm very happy to stay with you, and I'm not suffering. I'm very, very well. Don't worry about me."

In 1920 I visited Padre Pio for the first time with my family and a lot of people. I could still see at that time. His confessional was raised several steps. While he was hearing Confessions, he disappeared. Afterwards the people asked him where he went. He answered: "I flew over your heads." Maybe he was joking. Surely the people didn't see him leave, nor did I. The people think he went away by bilocation. I am sure he disappeared sometimes—not only once but many times. Padre Pio said that he went away because he wasn't able to breathe.

In 1927 or 1928 the people came near the church, and Padre Pio went out to visit with them. I was blind at the time. I asked him what we must do to be saved. He answered: "It is enough to observe the commandments of Our Lord and the precepts of the Church. That is enough to save the soul." He said: "If you don't become a very good Christian, when I go before Our Lady I'll accuse you, because you didn't tell the truth to me and to Our Lady, and therefore you didn't lie to me but to Our Lady."

When the people asked for something more, he always answered that we must pray, because he who prays is saved. When we asked him how we should pray, he answered: "We must pray with the heart and with the mind. It is useless to pray only with the heart without the mind." He also said that when we pray without attention, we will have the curse of the Lord; we will not be blessed, but the opposite—cursed. Therefore, when we pray, we must be very careful to pray with the heart and with the mind, with all our soul.

When the people said: "I can't pray very attentively," Padre Pio answered: "In this case, it is better that you go near Our Lord in the church without saying anything or doing anything. It is enough to give up the time for Our Lord. Our Lord is happy at least to receive us for the time we give up for Him."

He told us: "If anyone wants to become my spiritual child, he must live a very good life." He said that he offered to Our Lady all his sufferings and sorrows. He offered all those sufferings and sorrows with his prayers for all people.

Someone asked Padre Pio if he could become his spiritual child. Padre Pio answered: "To become my spiritual child, you must be a very good child of God. If you become my spiritual child without doing very well with God, it is useless."

26. Dorothy Valls
San Giovanni Rotondo

It was a labyrinthine road that led Dorothy Valls to Padre Pio from her home in Uruguay, to India, to Hong Kong, and thence to San Giovanni Rotondo. She is one of the approximately 150 persons or families who moved to San Giovanni Rotondo, drawn by the holiness and charismatic gifts of the Fourth Wise Man.—JS

* * *

I was born in Montevideo, Uruguay. Before I came to San Giovanni Rotondo on November 18, 1963, I was involved with yoga philosophy. I had been baptized but was not a practicing Catholic. In the course of my travels, which took me around the world, I first heard of Padre Pio from a lady in Guatemala.

I was planning a trip to the Orient, and I thought it might be better to see Padre Pio before I left. A friend in Milan told me: "It is difficult to see Padre Pio. Why don't you write to a hotel in San Giovanni Rotondo and ask them to arrange for your Confession?" I wrote but didn't get an answer. I decided not to go.

Through a Protestant girl from Switzerland I actually met Padre Pio. How I came to meet her was strange indeed. I was in New Delhi. She arrived there, too, and came to the same hotel as mine a half hour after me—even to the same room. The hotel manager said to me: "Please can you give the other bed which is in your room to this European girl, because we have no place for her?"

In the course of conversation she mentioned the name of Padre Pio. I jumped. I said: "Someone else has also told me about Padre Pio, but it is impossible to see him." She said: "How can you say that? I am a Protestant, and I have seen him." We did not pursue the conversation.

She told me that she would be in Banaras, India, on January 11.

I said to her: "I will try to be in Banaras too on the eleventh, so I can meet you." But I had no intention of meeting her. I wanted to avoid her, and she wanted to avoid me. So she went to Napal, and I went to Tripura, in completely opposite directions.

After two months I met her again in Hong Kong! We met in the same hotel on the tenth floor! It was a little hotel which had opened only five or ten days before. Nobody knew of it. After five days I met her in the corridor. When that happened, I understood that something supernatural was happening; I felt compelled to visit Padre Pio.

I came to San Giovanni Rotondo in 1965. On November 19 I went to Padre Pio's Mass, in order to discover the man of high spirituality for whom I had been searching. As soon as I saw him coming toward the altar, I began to feel moving air around me. I cannot say with precision what it was. It was something spiritual.

A dialogue started inside of me: "They say that there is no purity; he is purity. They say there is no love; he is love. They say there is no charity; he is charity." And so on.

In half a second I was absolutely sure he could not be wrong in his way of life and thinking. I realized: He is the truth, the final truth, and I must follow him. In that split second I was one hundred percent converted without any doubt of my new and beloved religion. It was an instantaneous conversion as soon as Padre Pio came into the church, as soon as I saw him. When he started the Mass, I was already a Catholic.

Since that day I have lived in San Giovanni Rotondo and have never had any doubts about anything. Previously I had not been going to church. When I was in Paris, if I was tired I sometimes looked for silence in a church, but not during services. A church or a mosque or a temple—all were the same. I believed in God and loved God very much, but I also believed in reincarnation. I was all mixed up. I was also following yoga philosophy, which I thought was very beautiful. But now I see that yoga was only a preparation; I find much more beauty in the Gospels. They speak of the love of God.

When I came here in 1963, I had the intention of remaining

only one or two weeks. I was tired of all my travels and was only looking for some rest. I thought that when I met Padre Pio, I would have a great disillusionment over him. But when I actually met him, I found that he was perfection, and this impression grew greater in my eyes as I got to know him better.

I decided to stay here. I didn't want to leave him for a minute. I was here for nine months with only one suitcase. Then my friend in Milan wrote to me and said that she was changing our apartment. So I had to go there to bring all of my suitcases down here to San Giovanni Rotondo. I didn't want to leave, not even for one day because for me Padre Pio was so precious. I was afraid that maybe I would lose what I had.

The young lady of whom I spoke, whom I had met in India and in Hong Kong, had come to San Giovanni Rotondo because of her attraction to Padre Pio. However, she had tremendous problems. On one occasion she tried to commit suicide. She took ninety pills. To make sure they all had their effect, she broke them up and swallowed them at one o'clock in the afternoon. Someone found her at four the next afternoon. She had also cut the veins in her wrist.

Her brain was completely destroyed. She was completely out of her mind. Then somebody brought her here, and through Padre Pio she recovered her memory and all of her mental faculties which she had lost completely. She told me that she was already at the door of hell, because she saw so many strange figures during the week before she recovered. Even though she was a Protestant, she was very grateful to Padre Pio. He gave her another chance to live.

She became a Catholic, but her problems continued. When she was in church, she thought Padre Pio was speaking with her spiritually. You could see that she was listening to someone, because the expression of her face changed. Maybe it was something diabolical. Then she would go to Confessiion and really talk to Padre Pio. But then, she said, what he told her was completely different from what the other person had told her "spiritually." She became angry with Padre Pio because he did not talk the same way the "other person" did in church.

For that reason Padre Pio always told us not to look for the unusual and the preternatural—it is very dangerous. A person might imagine it is Padre Pio talking to him, but it is someone else. The case of this girl is tragic, because again she attempted suicide, and this time she was successful. She is buried in the cemetery in San Giovanni Rotondo.

What he set for me is perfection, and it is perfection today. I will not do anything that Padre Pio did not like, even if it is as small as watching television. He did not allow me to buy a television set or go to the movies or to the beach. All those things were my life before.

He never comes into your house if you don't invite him. He respects your will very much. But the moment you say: "May I do this?" he would express his own opinion. No television and no movies! I never asked him about the beach, because I already knew his thoughts about that. Because they were not necessary for my health, I had to give them up.

He had his own standards of modesty which were very severe, and I think correct. Many times I get upset because I have watched television. All these things live in my brain, and sometimes I will pay the price for it even when I am at Mass. Padre Pio was completely right.

He wasn't an old-fashioned man. No, no, no. He had such a knowledge of the human soul that the great psychiatrists of the world like Freud could learn from him.

Padre Pio's campaign against short skirts started the year before the fashion began. He knew it was coming. We were there with normal skirts, and he sent us out: "Dress longer, dress longer." After a year everybody else had mini-skirts. If someone would wear short skirts outside and would come with very long skirts to his confessional, he would say: "Go away, clown!"

The graces Padre Pio obtained for me and my family are numberless. For instance, my aunt wrote to me: "Please speak to Padre Pio, because your uncle is in a mental hospital and has received nine electric shocks. His mental condition is hopeless."

In general, Padre Pio was against electric shock therapy. I spoke to him about my uncle, and he said: "In that way they make people crazy." I wrote to my aunt, saying that she should tell the doctors to stop the electric shocks. But another letter from her was already on the way to me. It wasn't an answer to my letter. She was already writing to me when I was writing to her. She said that the doctors suddenly decided to try a new method: that my uncle should go home and work. He had no other therapy. He is completely cured.

Two years ago I had definite symptoms of a tumor and was completely convinced I had one. I went to Confession and asked Padre Pio's permission: "May I go to the doctor, because I am afraid I have a tumor?"

He said: "Go to the doctor if you want to," but he added in a very low voice: "Don't worry, because you have nothing." I didn't go to the doctor. It was a false symptom.

Sometimes I laugh to myself when I remember the things he said. If I would repeat them to you, it would mean nothing, but the way he spoke was beautiful. For example, when I was working in the hotel, sometimes I couldn't sleep for more than an hour or two. So at Mass I became very sleepy. I said to Padre Pio: "I don't know what has happened, but I have such a temptation to sleep during your Mass." This was a serious problem for me, and I expected a profound answer from him. But he said to me with a very grave voice: "Do you know what to do?"

Full of expectation I said: "Please, Father, please tell me what to do."

He said: "Look. When you get sleepy, just stand up, so if you get sleepy again, you will fall over. Ho, ho, ho, ho!" I can't say it just the way he said it, but it left such a great joy inside of me.

He acted gently with me only when I was very depressed, almost at the breaking point. He didn't give candy to strong people. Someone asked him: "Father, why don't I smell your perfume any more?" and he said: "Why do you still need candy? Candy is for babies." These things were meditations for my soul. They gave me strength.

For me to be with his spirit is everything. I talk with him all day in my imagination—I need it. I feel it is my duty to remain here.

He led me here, and I am supposed to stay here, because he is my patron. He is the boss. I need him as a father and a mother. I live with the illusion that he is alive. I cannot change my love.

27.   Padre Marcellino, Capuchin
San Giovanni Rotondo

Padre Marcellino was a confrere of Padre Pio at the friary in San Giovanni Rotondo. I began by asking him what he thought was the most conspicuous trait of Padre Pio. —JS

*   *   *

He prayed for those who would come to know him. In the life of Padre Pio, nothing was extraordinary. What people considered extraordinary was extraordinary in Rome or in Milan, but not in San Giovanni Rotondo. Padre Pio often read souls; he read my spirit twice. But this is too personal for me to talk about.

When I was chaplain at a hospital in Milan, I used to bring Holy Communion to a man who had cancer of the throat. Occasionally I stayed with this man. He told me that when he went to meet Padre Pio in San Giovanni Rotondo, he arrived during the siesta hour. He rang the bell and a priest answered. He asked for Padre Pio, but the priest said: "Padre Pio is in his room. It is impossible to see him."

The receptionist allowed the man to wait for Padre Pio in the corridor. Just then Padre Pio was coming on his way to the chapel, but the man didn't recognize him. Padre Pio asked him: "What do you want?"

The man answered: "I want to meet Padre Pio."

Padre Pio said: "You must go away, because you are dirty [*sporco*]. I am Padre Pio, and you are very dirty."

The man said: "I thought Padre Pio was a saint, but I see that Padre Pio is rude."

Padre Pio said to him: "You must go away to prepare yourself to die." The man went away.

Three months later the man noticed something in his throat. The doctors said it was terminal cancer and wanted to operate.

The man returned to San Giovanni Rotondo, but this time he was ready to make his peace with God. After hearing his Confession, Padre Pio said to him: "You must not have the operation. You must not be touched."

The man lived eight years more. He died a friend of Padre Pio. He said: "I have received two miracles from Padre Pio. The second miracle is that I have lived for these past eight years, but the first miracle that I received from him was my conversion. He gave me faith."

28. Sister Pia of Jesus Crucified, O.C.D. Philadelphia, Pennsylvania

Sister Pia is now a member of the Order of Discalced Carmelites. Born in Philadelphia, she went to Italy to study art. Padre Pio's subtle but firm guidance led her to the Catholic Faith and then to Carmel. Antonio Ciccone, the artist of whom she speaks, has most graciously donated his beautiful drawings used on the front cover and frontispiece of this book.—JS

* * *

I came to know about Padre Pio when I went to Florence to study painting at the studio of Nerina Simi. There I met Antonio Ciccone, who is from San Giovanni Rotondo and has known Padre Pio all through his childhood. Antonio is an artist who is doing exceptional work on Padre Pio. I have seen no other artist able to capture Padre Pio with the sensitivity and skill of Antonio. Others fall far short.

One day Antonio told me about Padre Pio and gave me a photograph of him. I had never heard about anyone having the stigmata, and I was very impressed. I put the photo in the corner of my dressing mirror.

In this same period of my life I had begun an intense search for religious truth. I began to feel in my heart that I had found not only God's gift to humanity, Jesus Christ, but also the guardian of revelation, our mother, the Catholic Church.

Padre Pio's photograph remained tucked in my mirror, but other than thinking that he must be a holy man, I did not concern myself about him very much. First things first, and I had to solve the question of Catholicism. It was a serious and pressing matter in my life. I was not quite twenty years old at this time, and my family asked me to wait until I was twenty-one before I made such a drastic change in my life. I waited, and when I became twenty-one I was received into the Catholic Church.

In 1962 I settled in an attractive studio apartment in Florence to continue studying and painting. Louise, an American friend of mine, came to Florence that autumn and told me that she would like to visit Padre Pio. I felt drawn to accompany her: to spend a weekend there near that holy man, to unite my prayers with his, and to thank God for all the mercy and grace that God had poured into my life, especially for having brought me into the Catholic Church. So off we went by car, arriving late Friday evening in pouring rain.

My old friend Antonio Ciccone happened to be visiting his family in San Giovanni Rotondo at that time. When he saw that Louise and I were there, he went on his own and obtained reservations for us to go to Confession to Padre Pio the next day. When he presented us the slips with the reservation numbers I said: "I do not want to go to Confession to Padre Pio. That is not what I came down here to do. Padre Pio has more important things to do, and I do not feel any particular need to speak with him. I do not want to go!"

During the afternoon I was sitting in the church, reflecting on my life and all of God's goodness to me, when God bestowed upon me the enormous grace of a vocation to the religious life. It left me totally stunned, shaken, and lost.

I did not know where to go from there. I had never thought before of becoming a nun. My only consolation was that I had a reservation to go to Confession to Padre Pio the next day. I would tell him everything and he would be able to help me find my way. Now I was thankful beyond words for the opportunity which only that morning I did not care to take.

Louise and I were numbers nineteen and twenty for the confessional. That meant that we were the last two in line. Padre Pio heard only twenty women's Confessions each morning. That was the assigned lot. The twenty of us went into the old church and sat on benches in front of his confessional as we awaited our turn.

I had never had such a case of nerves—I was a wreck. My turn came and I stepped into the confessional. I began and said in Italian: "Father, it has been one week since my last Confession."

Padre Pio then said: *"Confessat"* [probably *Confessata*, meaning "You have already confessed"], or something like that, which was not clear to me. It was short and mumbled, and he spoke in his dialect.

Thinking that he had not heard or understood me the first time, I started all over again: "Father, it has been one week since my last Confession," and he mumbled what he had said before— something like *Sei confessat.*

I too repeated myself. I was determined to go on with what I had planned to say to him: that God now wanted me to enter religious life. I was hoping that Padre Pio would pick me up and give me some counsel and direction as to what I should do. Instead he said again what he had been repeating: *"Sei confessat!"* in a rather gruff manner. He brusquely closed the screen in my face as he turned to the other side of the confessional to hear Louise's Confession.

She began, and he closed the screen on her, too! She got up and left the confessional.

I was paralyzed with emotion and wonderment and could not for the life of me understand what had happened, or why Padre Pio had done that to me. I knew how far I was from holiness, but I had good will, enough to want to change, and I was not going to hide anything in my Confession. I knew that he had the reputation of reading hearts and that if the sinner was not going to mend his ways, he would often send him out of the confessional without absolution. That was not my case. I wanted help and direction, and yet he had walked out on me. And not just on me, but on both of us.

Anyone in the same position could have said: "I am finished with this." Louise was with me, and as soon as we walked out she said: "Let's get out of here. Let's go back to Florence. This is enough!"

I said to her: "No, we are not going until we find out what

happened, what went wrong." It did not make sense to me. I thought: "Well, if he is evasive, I have no intention of being so." I realized that God had new plans for me, and I needed Padre Pio's guidance, his spiritual help and experience; and I had enough good will to want to change my life.

Late that day we met Padre Eusebio and went through the details of the morning's encounter with Padre Pio. He said: "Oh, Padre Pio hears a person's Confession only every ten days. That is the custom here. When you said that it was a week since your last Confession, he was only trying to say: 'You have already confessed.' "

What a relief! I was perfectly at peace with that explanation and was content to return to Florence the next day as we were scheduled to do. I already had it in mind to return to San Giovanni Rotondo the following month and speak to Padre Pio then. I associated Padre Pio with the tremendous grace of my vocation to religious life. God could have enlightened me at any time or in any place, but he chose to wait until I had made that little visit to San Giovanni Rotondo where I would see such a radiant example of Christian sanctity shining in the person of the humble yet extraordinary Franciscan priest.

I returned to San Giovanni Rotondo the next month and then each following month until May. I was seeking my place in religious life. I did not know whether God wanted me to be a missionary, a nurse, a teacher with the Franciscans, the Dominicans, the Benedictines or what. In my Confession to Padre Pio each month I would discuss this with him.

He never said: "Go here or there, do this or that." He only told me to pray. That was the most precise direction I ever received from him. I would have loved for him to say to me: "Return to the States. Go to the contemplatives; that is what God wants of you," or some similar prophetic statement about my destiny. No, he only told me time and time again to pray, pray, pray. He made me do the work. I had to mature this way through prayer. I felt that this was the most important guidance of all. When he urged me to pray, I took him literally. I returned to Florence after each visit and I tried to do exactly as he directed me.

The trip from Florence to San Giovanni Rotondo took thirteen hours. I would get so excited that the hours flew by. It was never a difficult trip. I would think to myself: Look at this! What am I doing? This is the twentieth century, and here I am driving all the way from Florence to the southern part of Italy to see a priest who has such fantastic gifts from God. Two thousand years after the death of His Son, God raises up this miracle of sanctity for our modern world, and here I am driving down there. Me! All the way from Philadelphia! With a non-Catholic background!

It was an amazing experience even to think about it. I would think of Saint Peter and the other Apostles who knew Our Lord so well and who were close to Him, and I considered Padre Pio in the same category—as being an intimate friend of Christ. What a privilege to have the chance to go to see, and even to speak with such a person. And it was true! I was going!

As I passed through the modern outskirts of Rome with their many large apartment buildings, congested traffic and swarms of people going hither and yon, I always reflected on their numbers, compared to the very few who were with Padre Pio daily. Very few people, actually, stayed near him or even came to him. The gatherings outside the church doors in the morning were pushy enough, but they were a mere pinch compared to all the crowds in the cities as I drove south. I knew that God was at work and that his plan was unfolding.

In May I read a biography of Saint Teresa of Avila by Marcelle Auclair. Through it I arrived at the clear conviction that I had found my place. I was to follow the way of Saint Teresa in a life of prayer with the Carmelites. I had no doubt about it.

I immediately wrote to a priest in Philadelphia to find out whether there was a Carmelite monastery there. After I received a reply that there was, I returned to Padre Pio to tell him what had become so clear to me and to have his blessing or words of advice. When I told him that God wanted me to join the Carmelites and to return to Philadelphia, all he told me was: "Get on with it." I then asked him if I could have his blessing to remain in San Giovanni Rotondo until September so that I could be near him during those final months before I returned to the States. He gave me a simple "Yes."

I left San Giovanni Rotondo in September of 1963, thinking that I would never return. I had been told by many people that the Capuchin nuns were going to build a cloister in San Giovanni Rotondo and that I should join them. I certainly presented this suggestion to God in prayer. I knew that if I did, I would be close to the place and to the person from whom I had received so many of God's mercies and blessings. I felt strongly, however, that my place was in Philadelphia where I was to offer my life in prayer in a particular way for my family, for old friends, and for so many people who as yet did not know God's love and revelation. Certainly God had used Padre Pio as an instrument in my life but I believed that He would continue to lead me. I had to move on and trust Him.

During the ensuing months I took several courses in theology at Rosemont College, which was very near to where my mother was living. Christmas vacation came around, and I simply could not resist returning to San Giovanni to be with Padre Pio. Off I went for ten days, and then I did say my final goodbye. I was so happy to have had that little opportunity of seeing him again. I entered Carmel in June 1964.

[*I asked Sister Pia if she had ever experienced anything supernatural concerning Padre Pio.*]

I have never had a vision of him crowned with thorns or anything like that. I would see only the obvious physical expressions on his face: the glance or penetration of his eyes and especially the quality of his voice during the recitation of prayers. So many people have commented on the fervor of his Mass.

I was also equally impressed by the way he handled the monstrance for Benediction. I have never seen anything like it. He would be totally wrapped in worship. I do not mean in a trance, but I saw how aware he was of what he was handling. Often a priest will hold the monstrance with dignity, even giving a pause at the elevation for liturgical worship. One can sense the deliberate intention of the celebrant in doing this. But with Padre Pio it was much more than that—he radiated. The monstrance and he would glow as one. I was always very impressed by this. His voice, too, would have a quality of great depth and sincerity. It was this way day after day. He would be visibly moved by what he was saying. His emotion, gentle and penetrating, would fill the sanctuary. I always felt that each afternoon at Benediction the gate of heaven was being opened before us.

I never smelled roses, as many people have—only a rather inky scent coming from the wounds in his hands when I kissed them after Confession. His whole person spoke to me of holiness. Even had I not been able to go to Confession to him I would have benefited merely by being near him, to observe and learn from him. Holiness, love of God, union with God, prayer, sacrifice—all these things were evident in him. They emanated from him. How can I put it into words? It is impossible. No words are adequate.

I was learning how and what it was to be totally Christian, totally given to Christ. I saw a vivid example in Padre Pio of just that. He was raised up by God and given a special mission in the life of the Church. We each have our unique role to fulfill, and the extraordinary graces that were such a part of Padre Pio's life were not to be imitated or envied. What attracted me so much was the purity of the force of his love. I wanted to give my all, as he was giving his. The remarkable clarity of his life offered signposts, so to speak, for the journey.

You know that I had not been Catholic. For me the greatest blessing in this life is to be a Catholic: to have access to the fullness of the sacramental life of the Church, to be a member of the Church of Rome. Padre Pio's life was centered around his priestly ministry. All his time and energy went there. That was very clear, and that spoke out to me. Such a great man, and look where his choice lay! His Franciscan life shone out in all that it should have been: poor, humble, obedient. All these qualities and virtues I esteemed, and seeing Padre Pio helped me begin to sharpen my own priorities. In the face of Jesus on the cross, and in Padre Pio's wounds, God was telling us that it was all true.

Where does one go from there? Padre Pio showed us where—to a life given to the following of Christ. Participating and caught up in the life of the Church is where we are to find Jesus, renouncing all in the world that would lead us away from Him. The example of Padre Pio has taught us these things.

I see the life and mission of Padre Pio hidden in the mystery of Christ. With Padre Pio, God seems to be making another little breakthrough in our time, giving a reminder to everyone that Christ really lived and died on this earth for us. Padre Pio thought of nothing other than sending us back to Christ. Through Padre Pio we have another summons from God to believe in Christ, to believe in the Church and in the Sacraments. The fact is that Padre Pio was a priest and could stand before the people and call them to the Sacraments through his priestly function. That for me highlights the glory of his mission. I see his sanctity in that light.

Christ touched only a small number of people while he lived on earth. It was the same with Padre Pio. But the spiritual dimension of his life reaches to heights and depths which we shall never be able to grasp in this world. He was a saint with an immense and most unusual role to fulfill in the continued outpouring of Redemption won for us by Christ.

I truly believe this. We are touching here on the mysteries of God and of our salvation in Christ. To a point, we can be enlightened, but we must enter deeply into the arena of faith. God's mercy is beyond measure, and he lavished it upon us again by giving Padre Pio to our age. In heaven we shall see the how, why, and wherefore of all this. Now we must pray and reflect on what has been set before us.

[*I asked Sister Pia about her choice of the name Pia when she entered Carmel—and the second part of her name: Pia of Jesus Crucified.*]

Definitely I took the name Pia in his honor. I wanted to stay as close to him as I possibly could, and bearing his name would be a constant reminder. The name of his own blood-sister in the convent was Pia. I felt that by entering religious life, I was joining his family and I wanted his name.

In Carmel we also take a title. The crucifixion was the Christian mystery that has always meant the most to me. The fact that Jesus loved us so much as even to die for us on the cross tells me that His love is absolute. This is enacted in each Mass, and here we find Padre Pio again, offering and participating in this reality at the altar. So you see, I also chose the title of Jesus Crucified to remind me of what was and is most important to me. Thinking of Padre Pio only reminds me of Jesus and His great love that redeemed us.

As each year goes by, I realize more and more how tremendous Padre Pio was and is. I had the privilege of being with him so much during a certain period of my life, and all my hopes and ideals are bound up with him and what he exemplified. It is hard to put this into words, and I am forced back into prayer when I think about these things.

For myself, I cling to God's mercy. For Padre Pio, I sing God's praise and give Him thanks. Padre Pio is always standing before me, and his goodness puts me to shame. This is why when I think of him, I zero in on prayer again and ask God for His light and guidance to go on from there. Padre Pio sends me to prayer, and that is how it has been from the start: he directed me to prayer.

I do not know whether these were Padre Pio's exact words, but once someone told me that he said he only wanted to be a friar who prayed. Those words have inspired me in my Carmelite life. I can find in them the bare essence of what my vocation is all about. Here again he has been my teacher and my living example.

In 1965 I received a little message from Padre Pio through Padre Pellegrino. My translation is: "Tell her to keep herself burning ardently like a little lamp before Jesus in the Blessed Sacrament." I try to think of these words often, and they are always meaningful to me.

The Blessed Sacrament was probably the clinching factor in my becoming a Catholic. We do not have perpetual adoration in Carmel, but even in the solitude of the cell, adoration can penetrate walls and even the door of the tabernacle. We are so blessed to be living here under the same roof with His sacramental presence.

The exhortation from Padre Pio has given me a clear directive. Although I have always fallen far short of all that I should be and should have done, and I am always a beginner in all of these things, God has had mercy in the past and He will have it today. I sing a thousand alleluias about the wonders that He has done. In praising His glory and the glory of the saints, we too are lifted on high.

29. Padre Gerardo, Capuchin
San Giovanni Rotondo

With residence in San Giovanni Rotondo, Padre Gerardo is vice-postulator for the beatification and canonization of Padre Pio. As such he has the advantage of perspective: he can see Padre Pio's inner spiritual life without distraction which might come from Padre Pio's charismatic gifts such as the stigmata, bilocation, and miracles. I asked Padre Gerardo what he considers the importance of Padre Pio for people who have not had the good fortune of meeting him.—JS

* * *

Padre Pio has no importance to those who do not know him. If they want to know him, they must know his mission, his personality, what he said, and what he did. Faith itself comes from hearing (Romans 10:17). For those who know about him but have not seen him, it is probably the same as not actually having seen Christ.

For our greater inspiration, we must distinguish his social apostolate (that is, his charity) from his mystical life (his role as co-redeemer with Christ). With regard to his mystical life, we see an application of Saint Paul's words: "In my own body I make up all that still has to be undergone by Christ for the sake of His Body, the Church" (Colossians 1:24).

[To understand Saint Paul and Padre Gerardo's reference to Saint Paul, we must remember that Christ and Christ alone is our Redeemer. Christ is not a co-redeemer. Saint Paul teaches that we are co-redeemers with Christ if we suffer and die with Christ.]

Otherwise our sufferings have no value. The only explanation of suffering is union with Christ. Padre Pio gave himself as a victim soul to Christ. Padre Pio is the testimony of the Passion of Christ in the twentieth century of materialism and technological progress. Padre Pio is the heart of the Gospel—suffering and resurrection!

30. Canonization

The canonization process, through which a person is declared a saint, has evolved during the centuries. In the very beginning of the Church, Saint Paul applied the term saint to all Christians: "The household of Stephanas . . . is devoted to the service of the saints" (1 Corinthians 16:15). And to the Romans he wrote: "Look on the needs of the saints as your own" (12:13).

During the first three centuries of the Church, people associated the word saint with the martyrs, who chose death rather than betray their Christian faith. Then the people extended the term to other classes of people: holy men, women, and children, single and married, priests and laymen. Thus the saints were canonized by popular acclaim.

The voice of the people, however, was not always an accurate barometer of the holiness of their heroes. Some were later discovered to be less than shining examples of holiness, and sometimes unhistorical legends grew up around the people's choice.

So after several hundred years, bishops began to make their own inquiries. In the year 973, the Pope stepped into this evolving process of canonization. Pope Gregory in 1234 established a business-like procedure. Tighter norms were established by Popes Urban VIII (1623–1644) and Benedict XIV (1740–1785). Their procedures were incorporated into general Church law in 1917.

The Second Vatican Council did not deal directly with the causes of saints but mandated a revision of procedures. As things stand today, this is a very general sketch of the process of canonization of a saint:

1. Any Catholic person or group presents a petition to the bishop of the place where the holy person died. In Padre Pio's case, the petition was presented to Bishop Antonio Cunial on Novem-

ber 9, 1969, by Padre Bernardino Romagnoli, the postulator general for the causes of Capuchins. Twenty cardinals, two hundred bishops, and hundreds of thousands of laymen have petitioned Rome to declare Padre Pio a saint.

2. The bishop accepts the petition. In Padre Pio's case, on November 23, 1969, Bishop Cunial decided that it was "just and proper to ask the Apostolic See . . . to open or introduce the cause for beatification."

3. The bishop appoints an expert in theology, church law, history, and the practice of the Holy See, and contacts the Vatican's Congregation for the Causes of Saints. Archbishop Vailati, Bishop Cunial's successor, did this on January 16, 1973.

4. The Holy See gives clearance to the bishop to proceed. In Padre Pio's case, the Congregation for the Causes of Saints, on October 23, 1982, allowed Archbishop Vailati to pursue the cause.

5. The bishop appoints a promoter of the faith, popularly called the Devil's Advocate. He probes into everything and may introduce hostile witnesses.

6. The bishop consults the National Conference of Bishops and publicizes the steps taken, inviting people to testify.

7. The postulator submits a detailed biography. The preface of Padre Pio's official biography was written in 1974 by Cardinal Parente.

8. The bishop appoints censors to see if there is anything in the writings of the candidate against faith or morals. Their job will extend to 3,300 pages of Padre Pio's writings: his letters, talks, and school work.

9. Then the interview of witnesses begins. In Padre Pio's case, the interviews of ninety-three witnesses began on March 20, 1983. A solemn ceremony marked the occasion with an archbishop, nine bishops, 203 priests, and 20,000 laymen in attendance. Television cameras gave it national coverage. Since everyone connected with the interviews is sworn to secrecy, no progress report is presently available.

10. Then an investigation is made into an alleged miracle.

11. After all investigations have been completed, the Pope then

beatifies the candidate, that is, declares him/her a blessed. If the process continues favorably and another miracle is verified, the Pope at long last canonizes the candidate, that is, declares him/her a saint.

In the preface of this book I spoke of the visit of Pope John Paul II to San Giovanni Rotondo that is being planned for May 23, 1987. This visit will highlight the celebration of the one hundredth anniversary of Padre Pio's birth. I asked my confreres in San Giovanni Rotondo if the Pope might use this occasion to beatify Padre Pio. Their response, however, was negative, "because of the amount of work that still remains to be done." They do not expect the work to be completed before another year. Nevertheless, the visit of the Pope to San Giovanni Rotondo at this time, and his prayer at Padre Pio's tomb, remain highly significant events.

The most fitting epilogue that I can think of for this Padre Pio Profile is an excerpt from the letter that the National Conference of Polish Bishops sent to Pope Paul VI, petitioning him to canonize Padre Pio. Karol Wojtyla's name, as I mentioned in the preface of this book, was second among the signatures.

> All of us are convinced of the holiness of Padre Pio's life and special mission. Proof of this is his exemplary life replete with virtues, especially his continuous prayer with special devotion to the Passion of Our Lord Jesus Christ and the most Blessed Virgin Mary. Another proof is his life of penance, with various heroic sacrifices and admirable love of God and neighbor in the apostolate reaching into the whole Christian world, even into Poland.
>
> Today, when many people frequently stray from the truth and from religious life, from a religious apostolate, and from the dignity and ministry of the priesthood, Padre Pio was a priest and religious of our time. He is a shining example to a world in turmoil.
>
> The Vatican Council demands that religious engage in an apostolate "especially which promotes prayer and good example" and that they "cooperate with the bishops for the good of souls." These attributes are clearly manifested in Padre Pio. He "became a prayer." We consider it opportune that his cause for beatification and canonization be introduced.

Postscript

Pope John Paul Visits
Padre Pio's Crypt and Hospital

In the preface of this book I mentioned that Pope John Paul II was planning to visit San Giovanni Rotondo. We have stopped the presses on *A Padre Pio Profile* to include this late report of the Pope's visit on May 23, 1987. In its June 6 issue, the English edition of *L'Osseratore Romano* gave the event more than a full page coverage. The worldwide significance of the Pope's visit, and the space given it in the Vatican press, can hardly be exaggerated. Here are a few excerpts of the Pope's message at the shrine of Our Lady of Grace. I consider them only a breath short of canonization of Padre Pio.

This sacred place has certainly been the hub of great spiritual radiation in recent times, thanks to the work of Padre Pio. He offers us even today a point of reference. Were not the altar and confessional the two poles of his life? This priestly witness contains a message as valid as it is timely . . . Those essential and perennial values of the priesthood were realized in an excellent way in Padre Pio.

Who does not recall the fervor with which Padre Pio relived the Passion of the Christ in the Mass. . . . For him, the Mass was the fount and culmination, the hub and the center of his whole life and work. This intimate and loving participation in the Sacrifice of the Cross was the source of Padre Pio's dedication to and availability for souls. . . . This is so well known that I do not intend to dwell on it.

How lively was his sense of justice and mercy, his compassion for those who suffered, and how concretely he committed himself to helping them. I wish to thank the Lord with you for having given us dear Padre Pio, for having given him to our generation in this very tormented century. In his love for God and for his brethren, he is a sign of great hope.

Additional information and material
on Padre Pio may be purchased from:

Mrs. Vera Calandra
National Center for Padre Pio, Inc.
2213 Old Route 100
Barto, PA 19504